Depicting the Colours in Water

SCHOOL OF COLOUR PUBLICATIONS
www.schoolofcolour.com

by Craig Letourneau
and Michael Wilcox

ISBN 1-931780-10-2
Text, Illustrations and Arrangement Copyright:
The Michael Wilcox School of Colour Publishing Ltd.
Gibbet Lane, Whitchurch
Bristol BS14 OBX
England
Tel: UK 01275 835500
Facsimile: UK 01275 892659
First published 2002

Distributed in the UK, EEC and associated territories by:
Search Press Limited
Wellwood, North Farm Road
Tunbridge Wells, Kent
TN2 3DR, England
Tel: (01892) 510850
Facsimile: (01892) 515903
Email sales@searchpress.com
Website www.searchpress.com

Distributed to the trade and art markets in Australia by:
Keith Ainsworth Pty Ltd
Unit 6/88 Batt Street
Penrith NSW 2750
PO Box 6061
Tel: 02 47 323411
Facsimile: 02 47 218259
Email: ainsbrook@ozemail.com.au

Scanning and colour balance:
Paul Goodman
Planning:
Matthew Brown
Page design and layout:
Paul Goodman
Finishing:
Maureen Bonas
Artwork:
Craig Letourneau
Text:
Craig Letourneau
and Michael Wilcox
Coordination:
Anne Gardner
Printing:
Imago productions F.E. Singapore
Print coordination:
Emma Bell and Desmond Heng

Contents

How to use the swatches

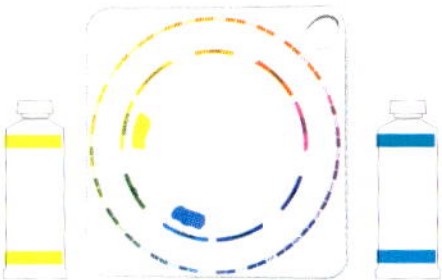

Hansa Yellow and Cerulean Blue

A range of bright greens which vary in transparency from the semi transparent green-yellow to the opaque green-blue.

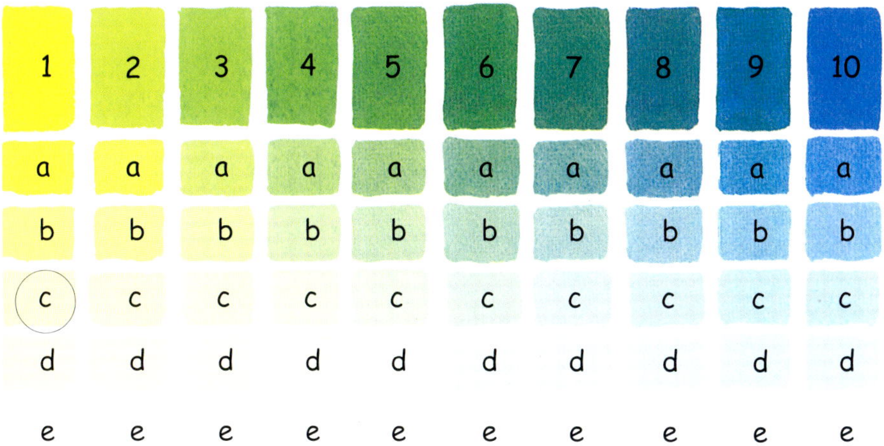

Throughout this publication we will be referring to the *Colour Mixing Swatch Book*. As mentioned on the back cover, you will need this publication in order to obtain the most from this and other titles in the 'Colour Notes' series.

In the example above, (which can be found on page 9 of the *Colour Mixing Swatch Book*), numbers and letters have been assigned to each hue for ease of identification.

The page number in the book is shown first, in this case 9. This is followed by the numbered colour from the top row and then the lettered tint (where applicable). Therefore, colour 9/1c is to be found on page 9. After finding page 9, go to the colour numbered 1 (top left), then down to C. This colour, 9/1c, has been circled above.

Please take a few moments to familiarise yourself with this system as we will be using it throughout the book.

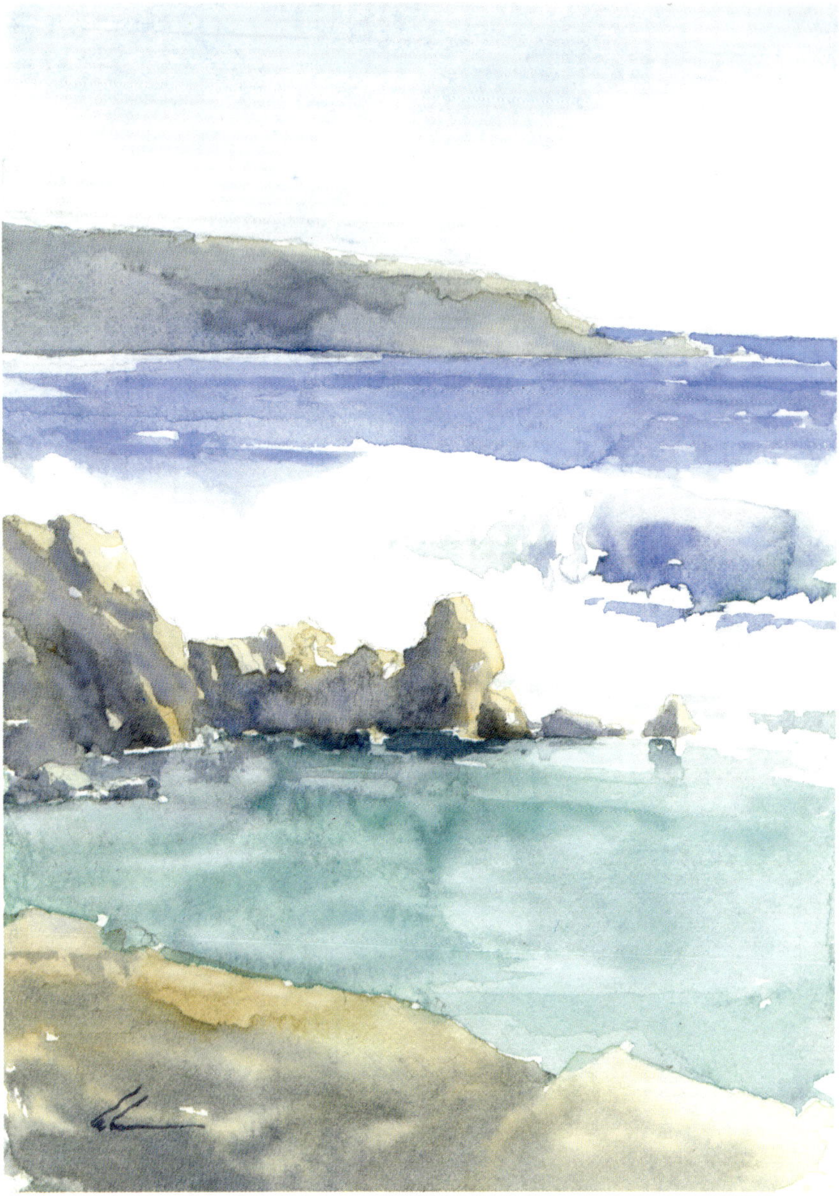

The colour of water

Artists have always been drawn to the sea as it offers unparalleled painting opportunity. One can spend a lifetime not only enjoying the subject but also trying to understand how to paint it.

The colours that we perceive are derived from the lighting, shadows and whatever lies beneath the surface.

Compounding the situation is the ever changing, ever moving nature of water. If we follow a few basic rules, which will apply in general to the nature of water, we can avoid mistakes and learn by observation.

1) The deeper the water becomes the darker it appears. Light has a difficult task penetrating deep water, hence its dark value.

2) Shallow water allows the light to bounce off the bottom surface giving lighter values.

3) The darkest value of water can usually be found at the horizon.

In this painting the distant water was painted in a graduated wash of Ultramarine Blue and Cerulean Blue, darker at the horizon. The foreground water was painted with Cerulean Blue and Phthalocyanine Green in a much 'warmer', lighter value. The darkest values in the water appeared close to the rocks where they were in shadow.

Cerulean Blue and Ultramarine P49
9d 9e

Cerulean Blue and Ultramarine P49
10b 9b 10c

Raw Sienna and Ultramarine P19
7c
3d
8b
2d
8c

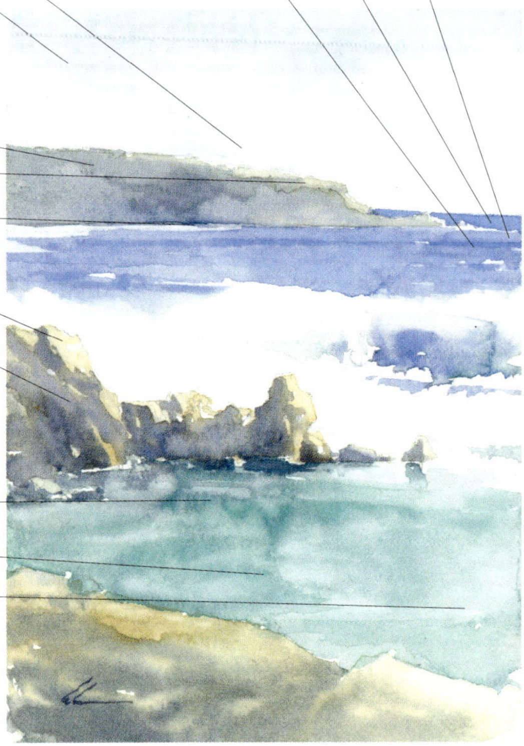

9b
7b
5d
Cerulean Blue and Phthalocyanine Green P16

Water can come in a diverse array of colours depending on the many factors affecting it. This small, simple study shows a rich blue sea, appearing darkest at the horizon. Then, as it approaches the shallow foreground, it appears lighter and greener. The result of sunlight passing through and reflecting off the sandy bottom.

The colour of water

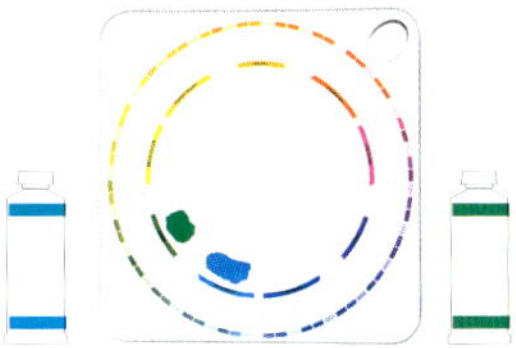

Page 16 of the Colour Mixing Swatch book.

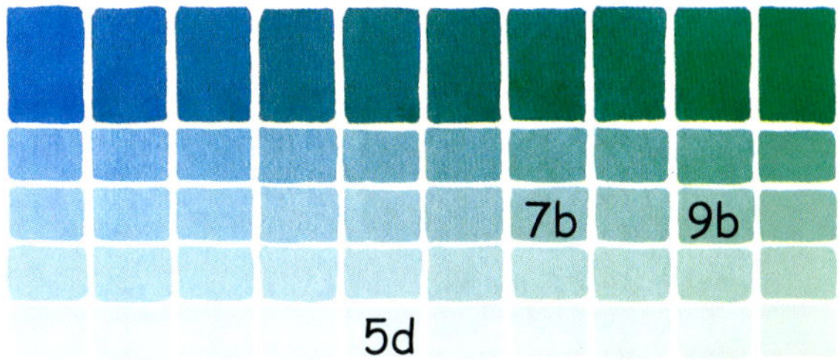

Cerulean Blue and Phthalocyanine Green

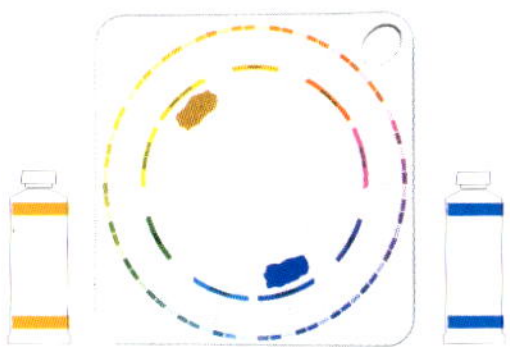

Page 19 of the Colour Mixing Swatch book.

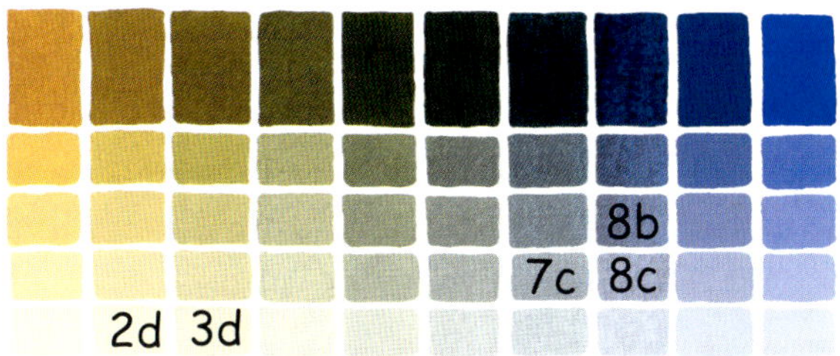

Raw Sienna and Ultramarine

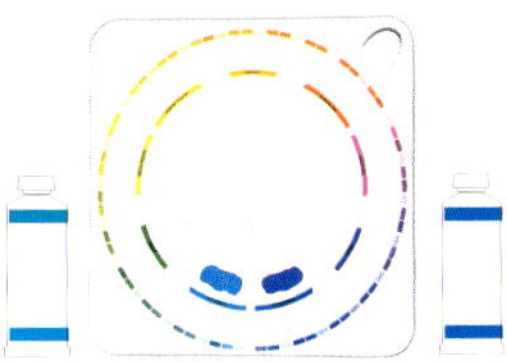

Page 51 of the Colour Mixing Swatch book.

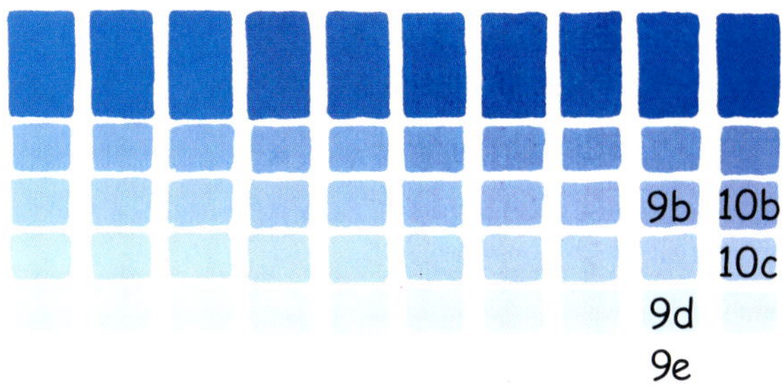

Cerulean Blue and Ultramarine

The above colour swatches will help you to become familiar with the outline given on page 3. With a little practice you will be able to quickly find any required mix from the *Colour Mixing Swatch Book.*

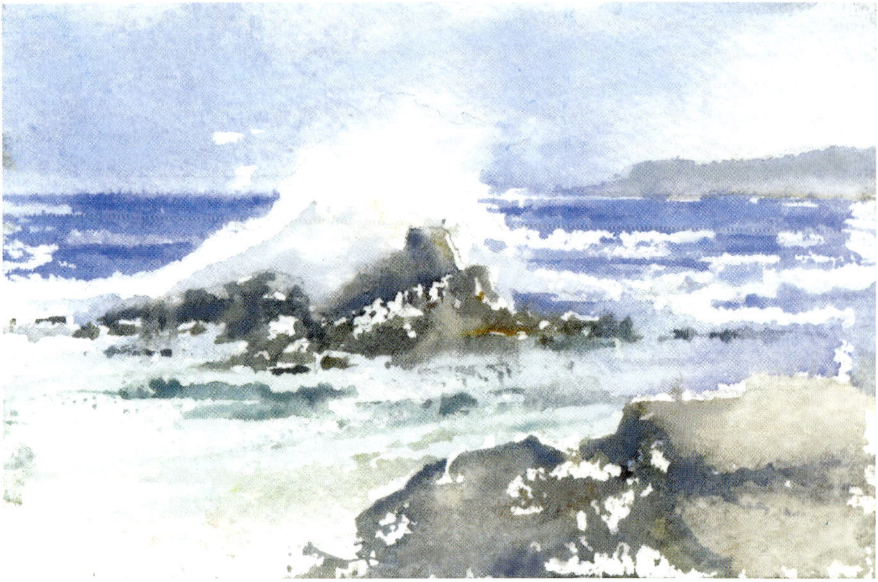

Breaking waves have always been a favourite subject for artists.
In this simple study, I allowed the white of the paper to become the lightest value of the wave.
After beginning the painting with an Ultramarine Blue and Cerulean Blue sky, I then painted the darker values of the background water from the same range of mixes. Various blends of Phthalocyanine Green and Ultramarine were used to create the foreground water. All the rocks and land masses were painted with Mixed Bright Orange and Cerulean Blue and the same orange and Ultramarine for the darker values. The shadows under the waves were painted in pale 'coloured greys' produced from mixes of Bright Orange and Cerulean Blue.

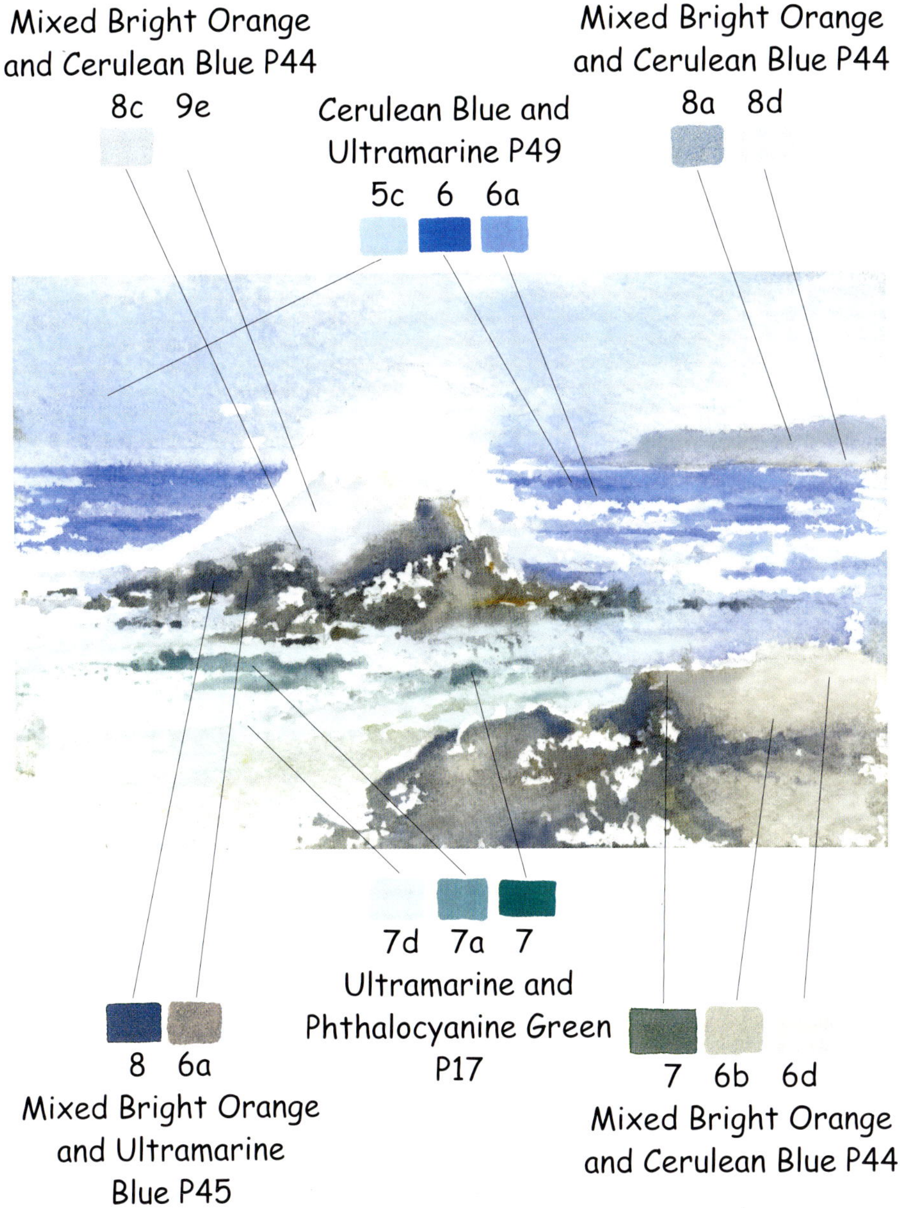
Mixed Bright Orange and Cerulean Blue P44
8c 9e
Cerulean Blue and Ultramarine P49
5c 6 6a
Mixed Bright Orange and Cerulean Blue P44
8a 8d
7d 7a 7
Ultramarine and Phthalocyanine Green P17
8 6a
Mixed Bright Orange and Ultramarine Blue P45
7 6b 6d
Mixed Bright Orange and Cerulean Blue P44

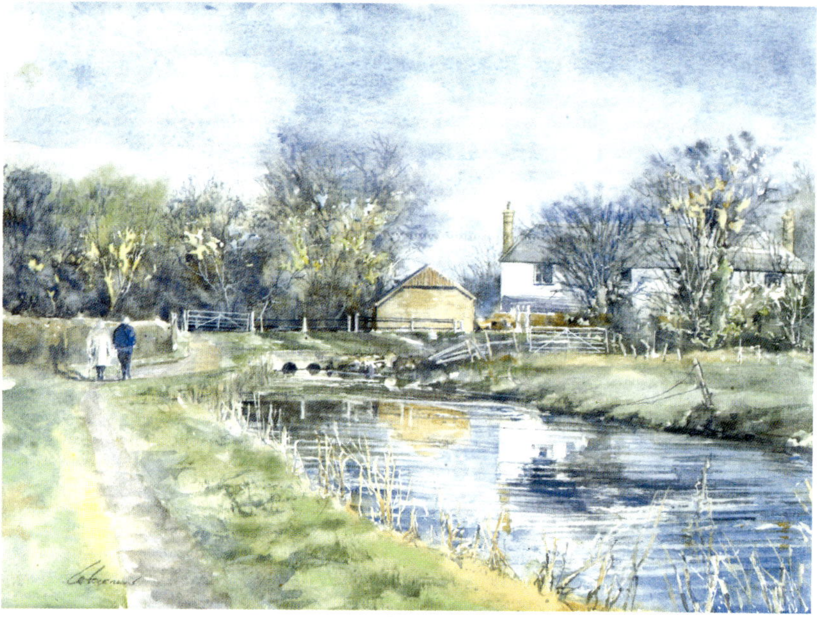

I started with a wash to both the sky and water using Cerulean Blue. Whist wet, Ultramarine was added to the upper areas of the sky for more interest. I was careful to leave the sky and water light, so that high contrast would be a key element in the painting. With the sky and water still wet, I quickly added the background trees using mixes of Cadmium Yellow Light and Ultramarine Blue. It does take a little practice to know how wet the sky should be to achieve subtle colours and blends without becoming muddy. I built up my water in layers using blends of Ultramarine and Cerulean Blue, taking care to let each application dry thoroughly. A natural sea sponge was then used to soften any hard edges.

Cadmium Yellow Light and
Ultramarine Blue P12

9b 9 4a 1c 6

Raw Sienna and
Ultramarine Blue P19

2b 2d 2c 2 9 2a

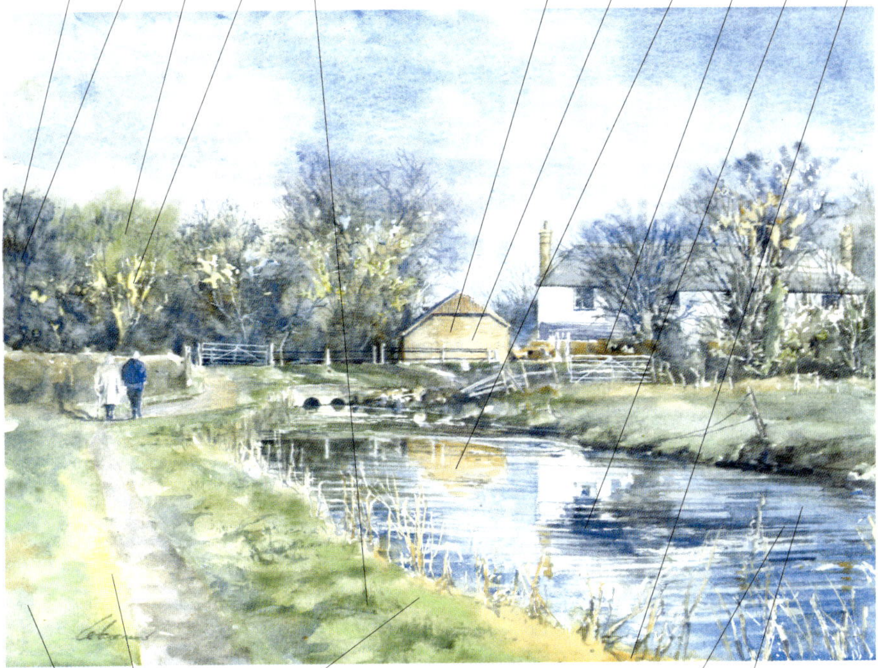

5c 1b 4a

Hansa Yellow and
Cerulean Blue P9

8b 8d

Cerulean Blue and
Ultramarine Blue P49

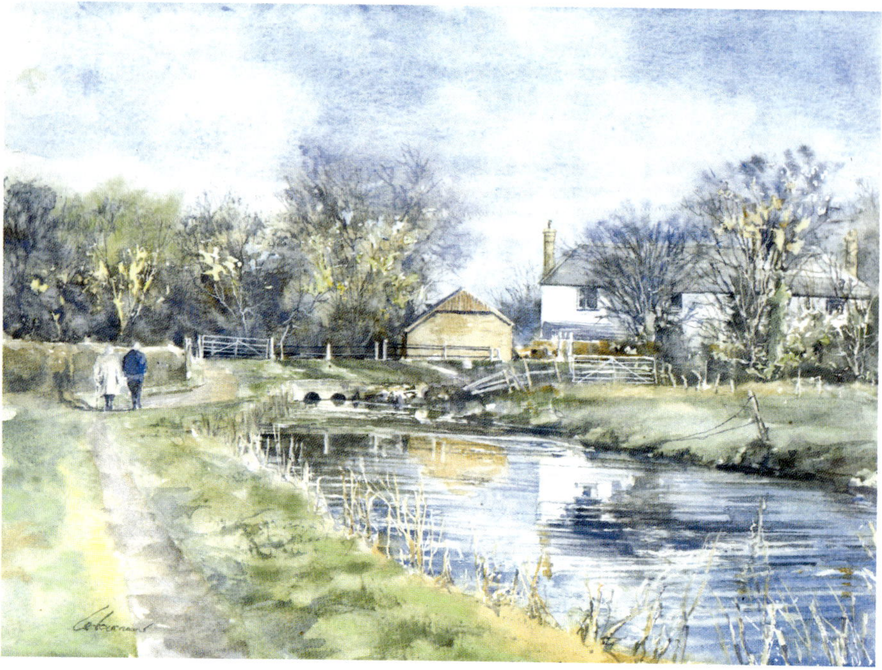

Although I try to leave the white of the paper untouched where fences and weeds will be shown, it is not always possible. So I used a little white mixed with Raw Sienna or Yellow Ochre to paint in, or tidy up, the fences and weeds. The grasses were painted using Hansa Yellow and Cerulean Blue. The 'warm' pale orange colours of the barn stand out as the complement of the 'cool' blue water. A pathway was painted as the grass was nearly dry, giving soft edges.

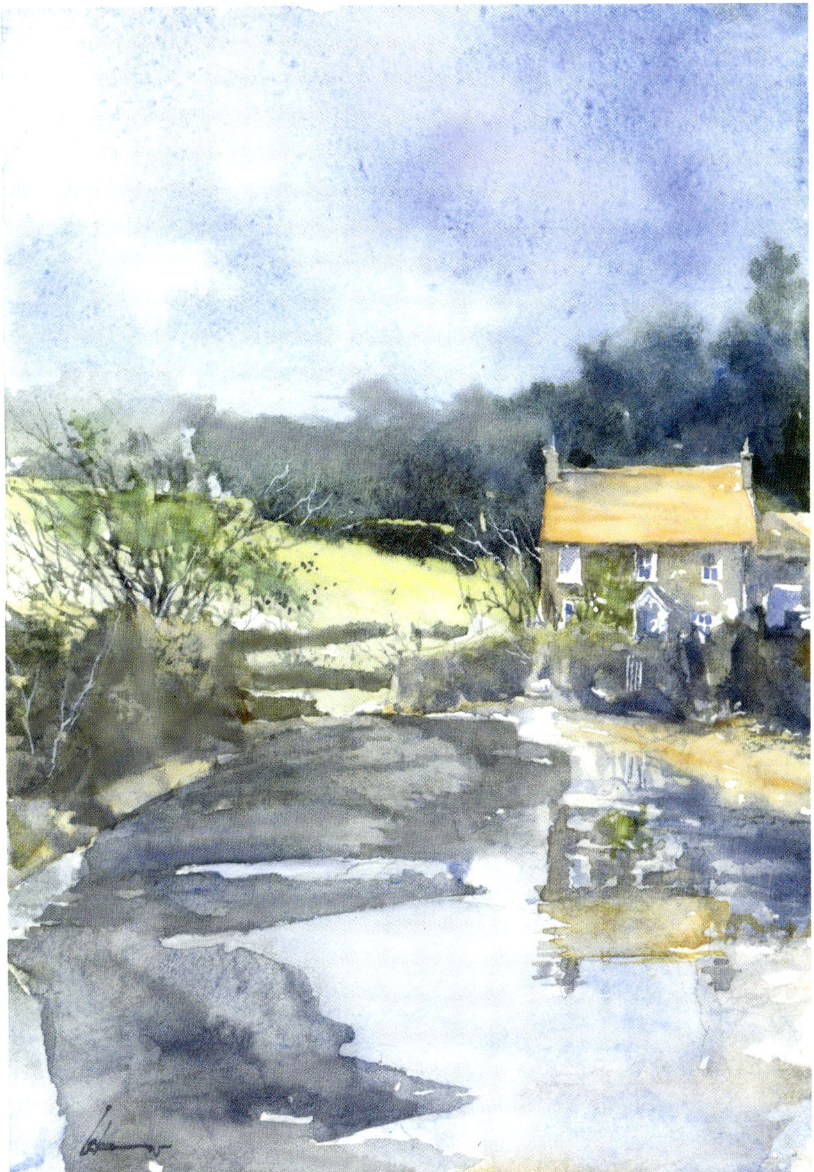

Standing water

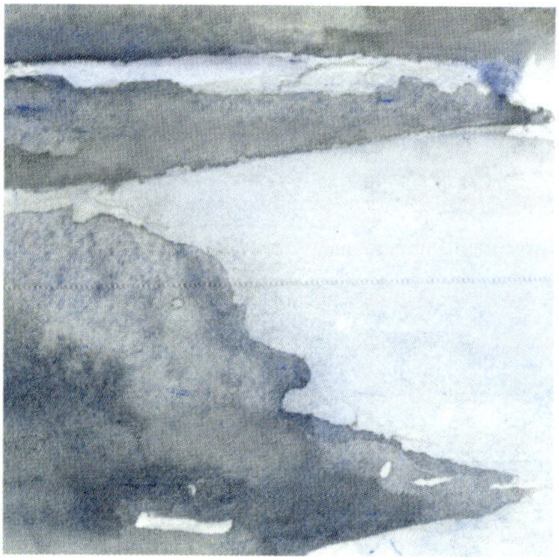

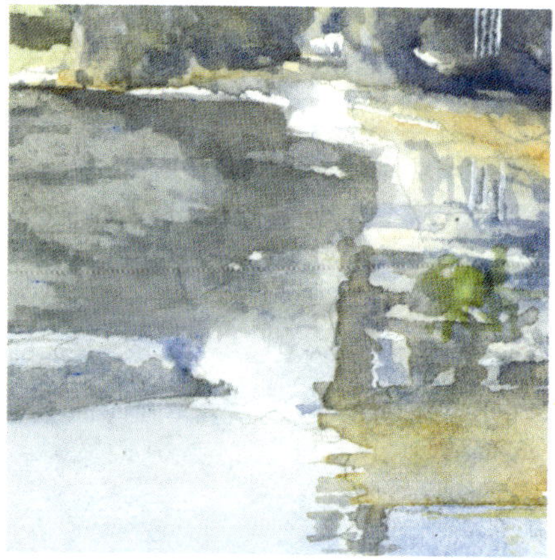

Puddles, or standing water, have reflective properties which can help to unify a scene. In a painting, they allow the artist to bring the sky colour down to the foreground. This often helps to balance the work.
The reflections, however, may appear exaggerated as value qualities change; light objects might appear lighter in reflection and dark objects, darker. In 'Standing water' I used Ultramarine Blue slightly modified with Burnt Sienna to loosely paint in the sky and puddle. The background trees were then painted in stronger mixtures of the two and allowed to blend into the sky. When dry, the background greens were painted using Hansa Yellow and Cerulean Blue. A Raw Sienna & Ultramarine mix was also used in the foreground. The hedgerows were painted with Raw Sienna & Ultramarine Blue.

Standing water

Hansa Yellow and Cerulean Blue P9

4a 5a 2b

Ultramarine and Burnt Sienna P48

5c 10d 10b 7a 10d

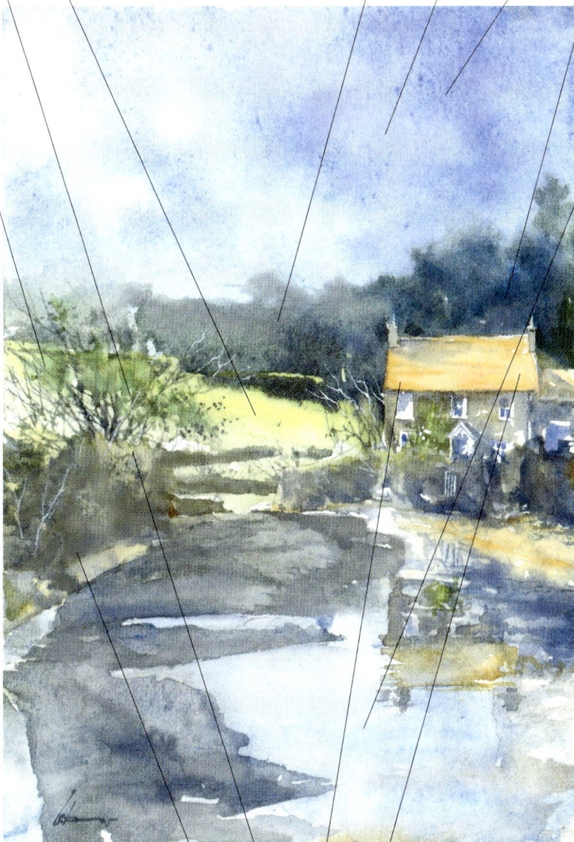

6a 4c 1a 1c

Raw Sienna and Ultramarine P19

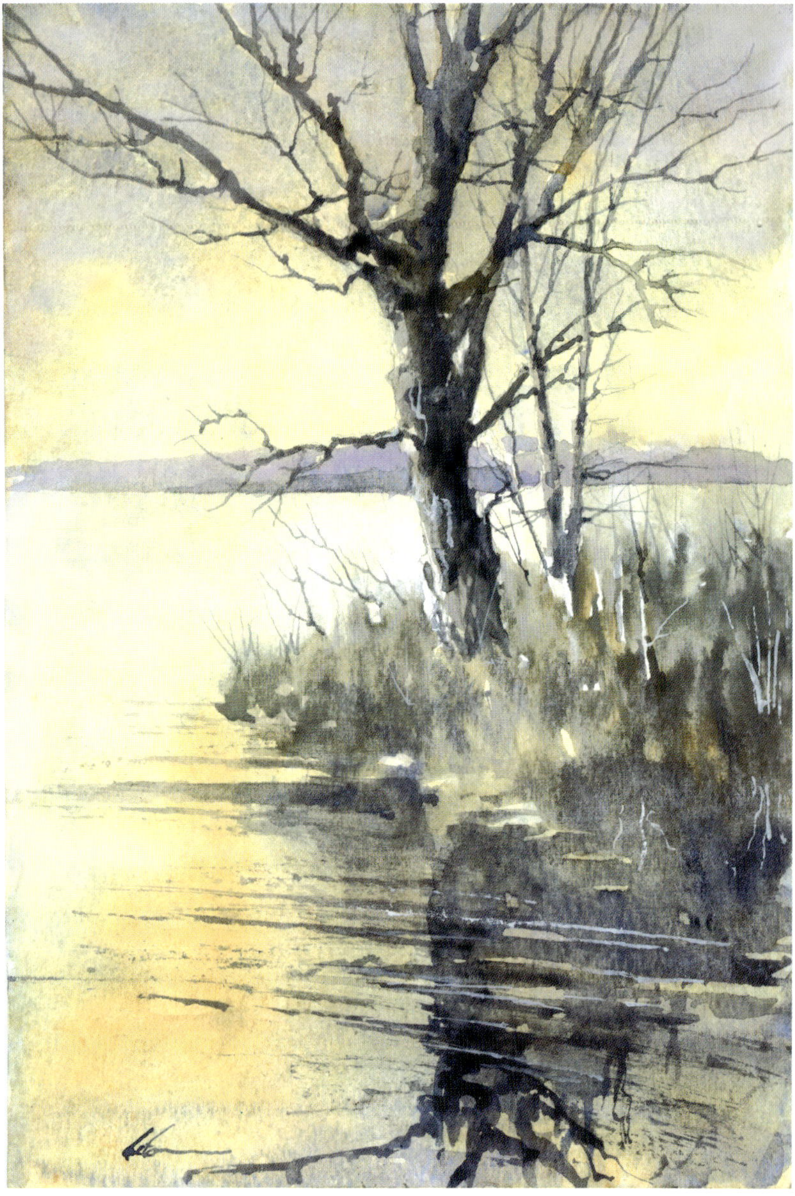

Hansa Yellow and Raw Sienna P22

5d

10b

Ultramarine and Quinacridone P22

5c 5b 9c

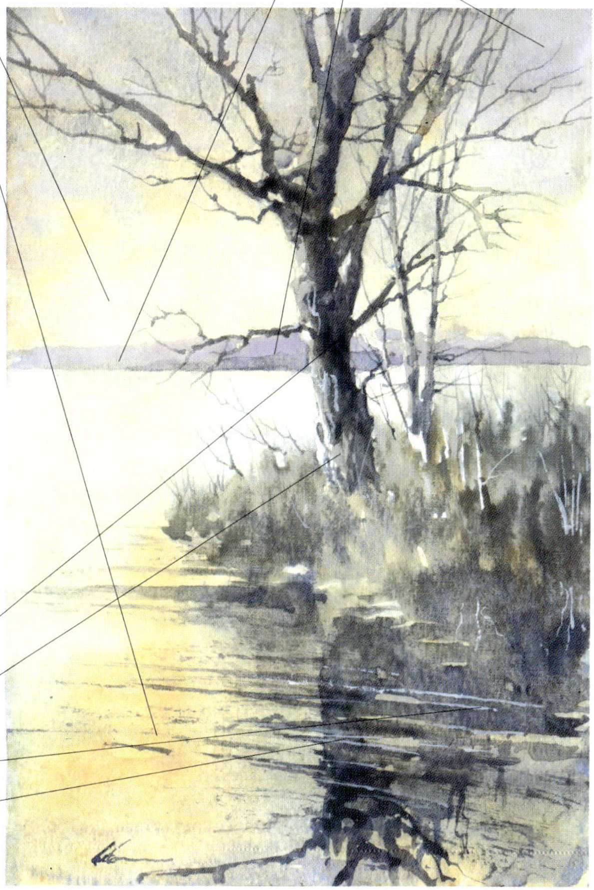

6

6d

10c

6b

Ultramarine and Burnt Sienna P48

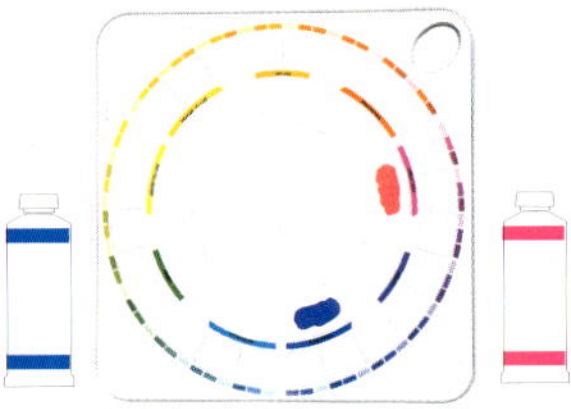

Page 22 of the Colour Mixing Swatch book.

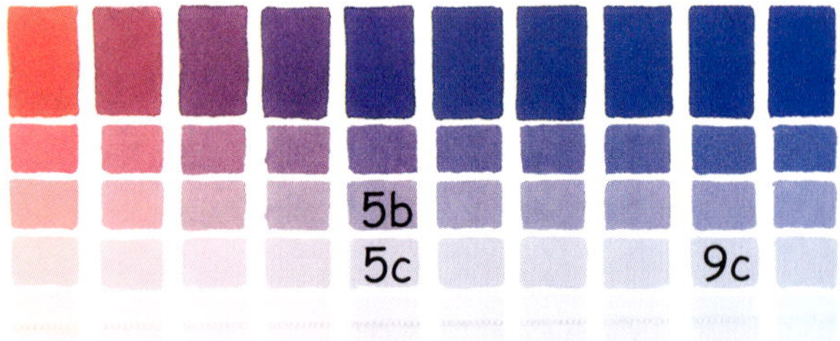

Ultramarine Blue and Quinacridone

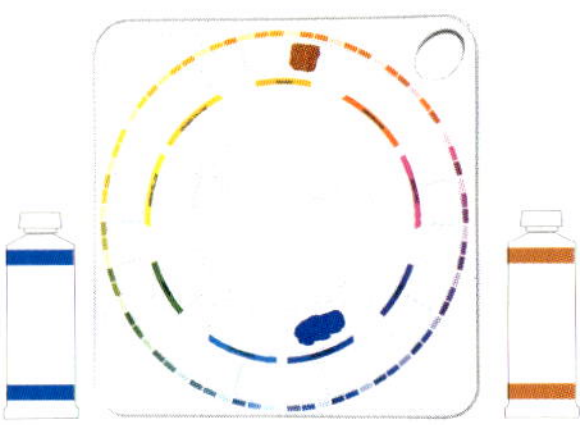

Page 48 of the Colour Mixing Swatch book.

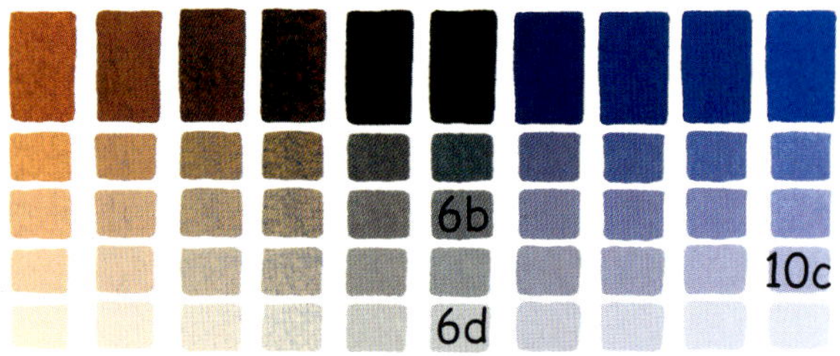

Ultramarine Blue and Burnt Sienna

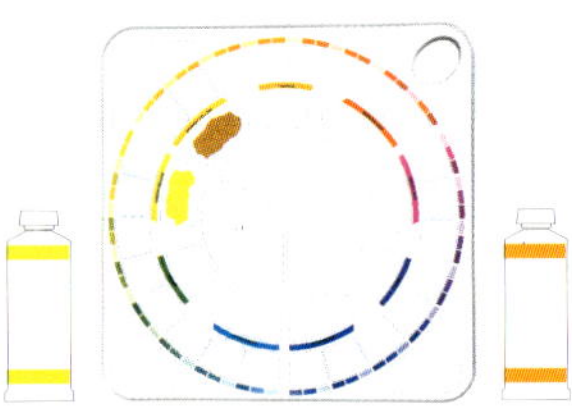

Page 53 of the Colour Mixing Swatch book.

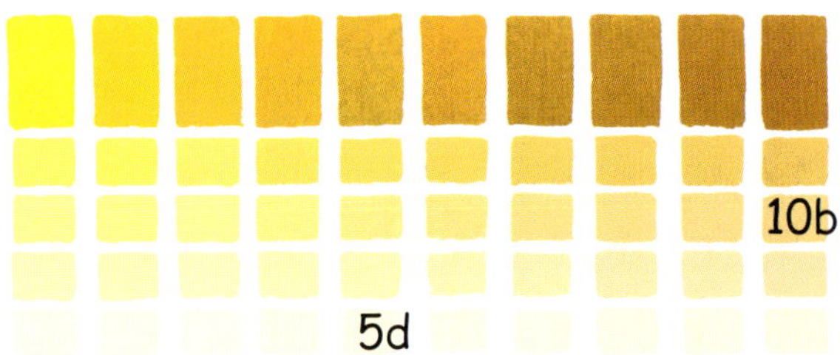

Hansa Yellow and Raw Sienna

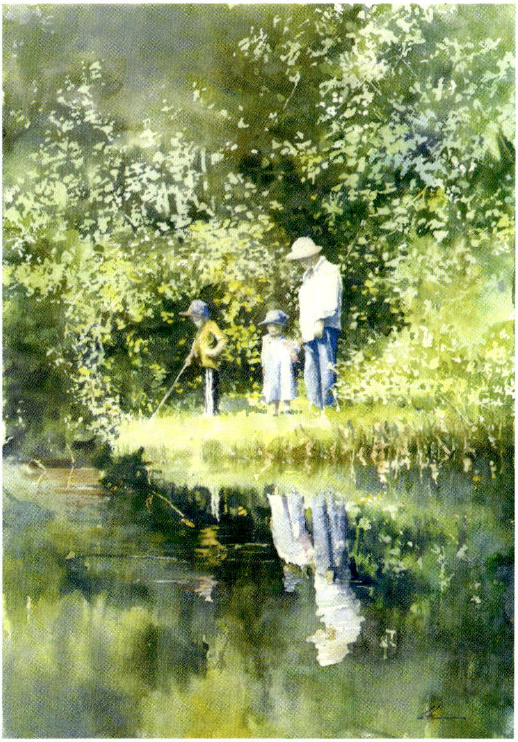

I began by masking the figures and highlights of the foliage with masking fluid. This allowed me the freedom to develop deep, dark washes and still render a delicate scene. Mixes of Phthalocyanine Blue and Hansa Yellow provided bright yellow greens. Quinacridone Violet and Phthalocyanine Green gave the deeper greens. When the mask was removed I painted in the 'saved' areas.

Phthalocyanine Blue and
Hansa Yellow P13

2 3b 10c

Quinacridone Violet an
Phthalocyanine Green P

6b 6a 6 9b

Mixed
Orange and
Cerulean P44

1b

4b

4

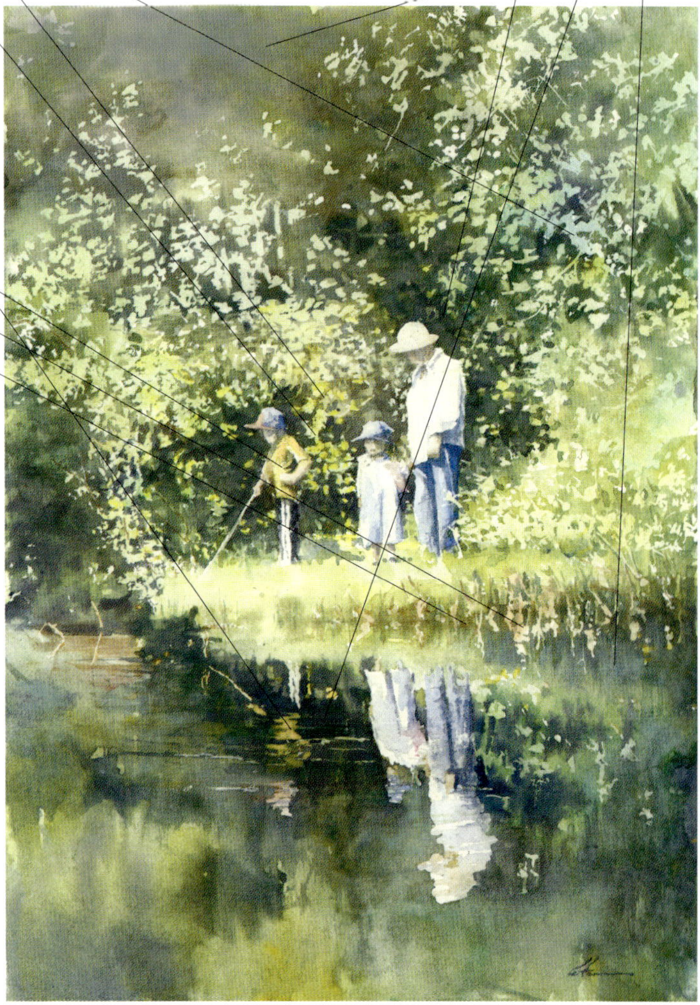

Still water

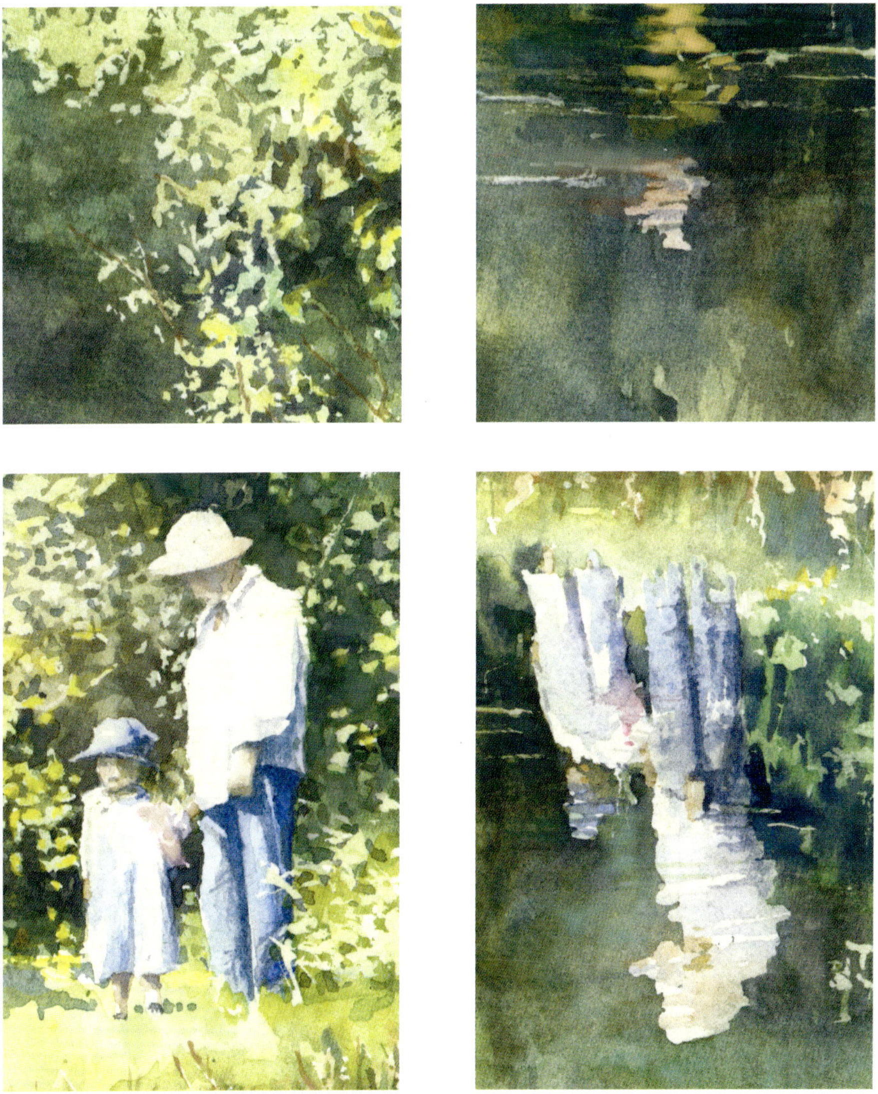

A light application of masking fluid will allow deeper, 'background' colours to be applied freely.

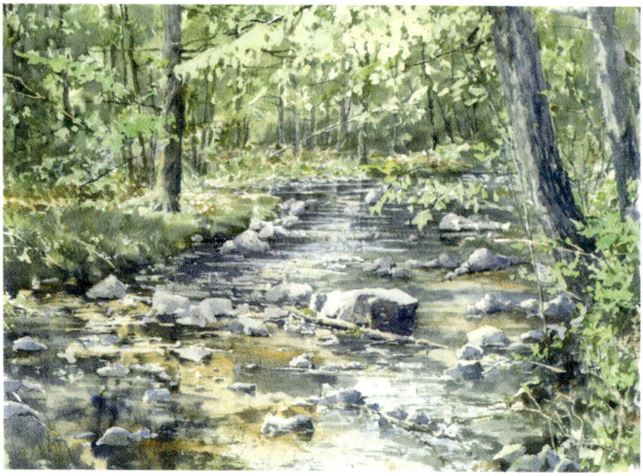

To convey the feeling of moving water, I wanted to use expressive, flowing strokes. This was best achieved by masking certain areas first. I applied masking fluid where the rocks, sticks and highlights in the water would be.

Masking fluid is best applied with a disposable brush, or one that has been soaked in undiluted washing up liquid and used solely for this purpose. Dry fluid can never be totally removed without harming the qualities of the brush. When dry, the mask was removed and the white of the paper could be tinted, adding valuable highlights.

Editors note: This book is intended to give guidance for all media; watercolours, oils, acrylics etc. Where the use of masking fluid is suggested the advise is only applicable to watercolour paints, gouache or perhaps when working in thinly applied acrylics.

River water

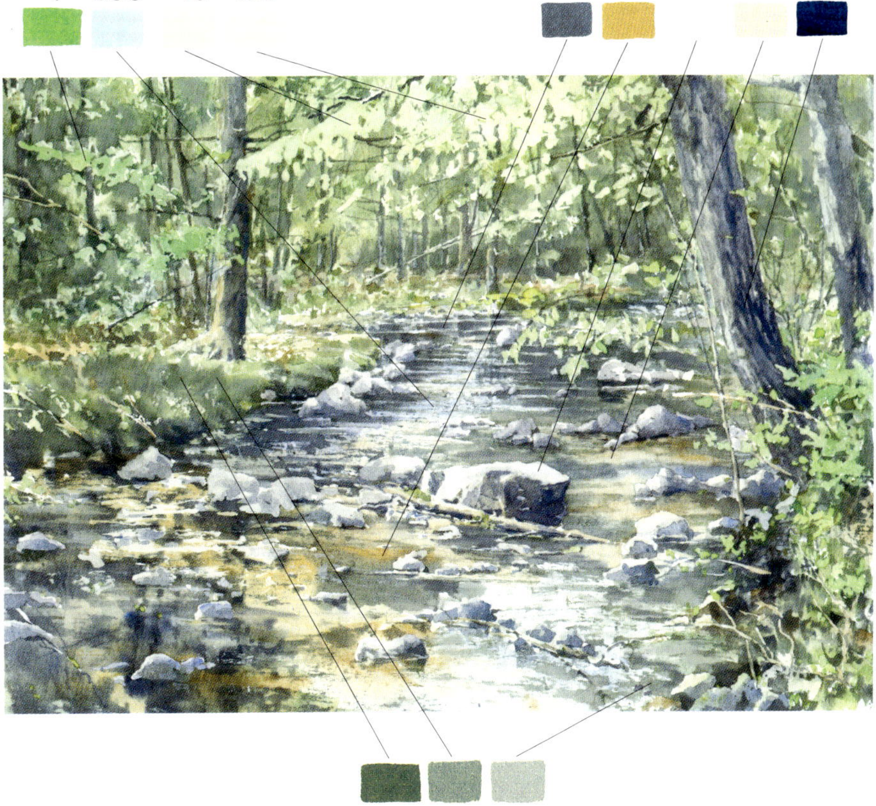

Cerulean Blue and Hansa Yellow P9
4 10c 4c 2d
Raw Sienna and Ultramarine P19
7a 2a 7e 3d 8
7 7a 7b
Cad Yellow and Ultramarine Blue P12

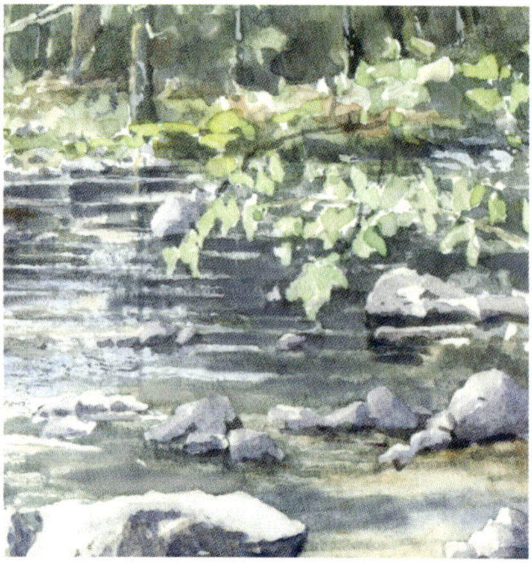

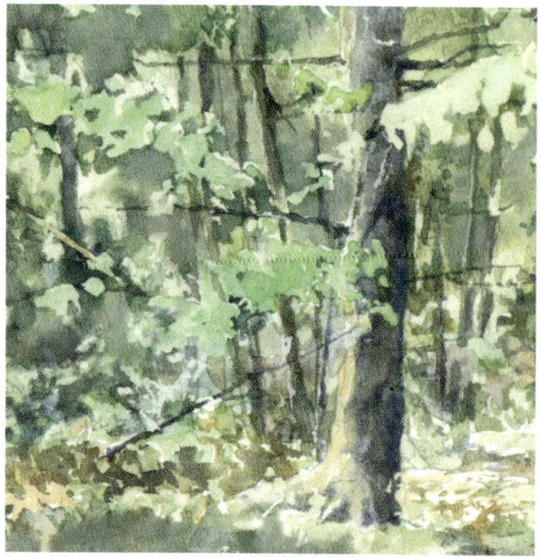

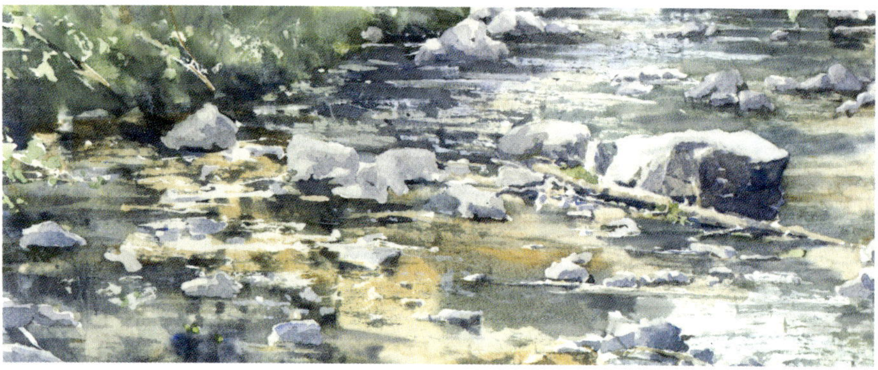

As with all of the paintings, only the more important mixes have been identified. To show all of the combinations would be impossible. If producing these paintings yourself, you will find the other mixes on the relevant colour mixing swatches. Many are simply lighter or darker versions of the identified colours.

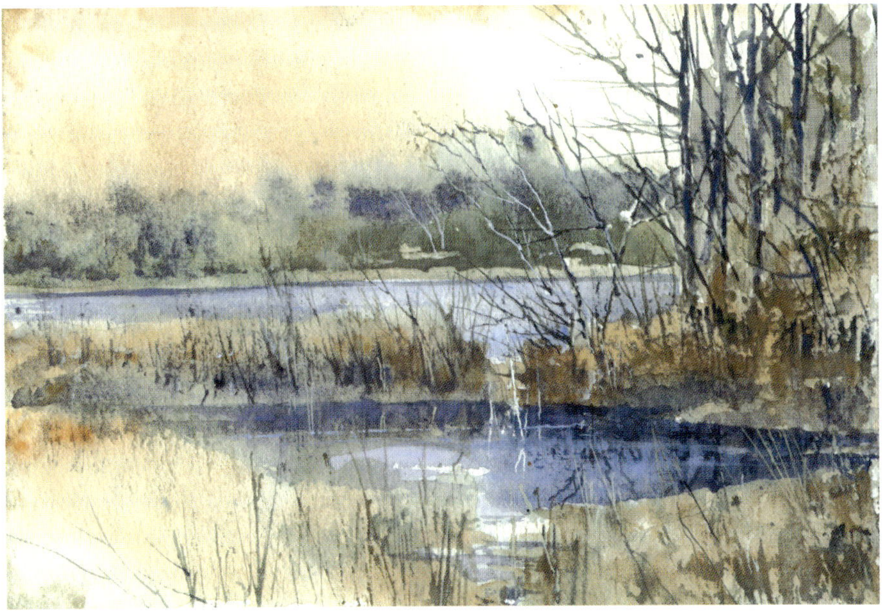

This wooded pond scene has a foreground area of shaded water that appears darker and more vibrant than the distant stretches. I used Phthalocyanine Blue and Burnt Sienna for its darkest areas. The distant water was painted with Cerulean Blue and Phthalocyanine Blue.

Raw Sienna and Ultramarine Blue created the sky, the bare trees and the foreground plants. Notice the incredible range possible from just two colours. Using such a combination for much of a painting helps to create colour harmony. A combination of Cadmium Yellow Light and Ultramarine Blue was used for the distant evergreen trees.

Pond water

Cadmium Yellow Light and
Ultramarine Blue P12
7 7a 7b

Raw Sienna and
Ultramarine Blue P19
2c 2e 1 2a 3

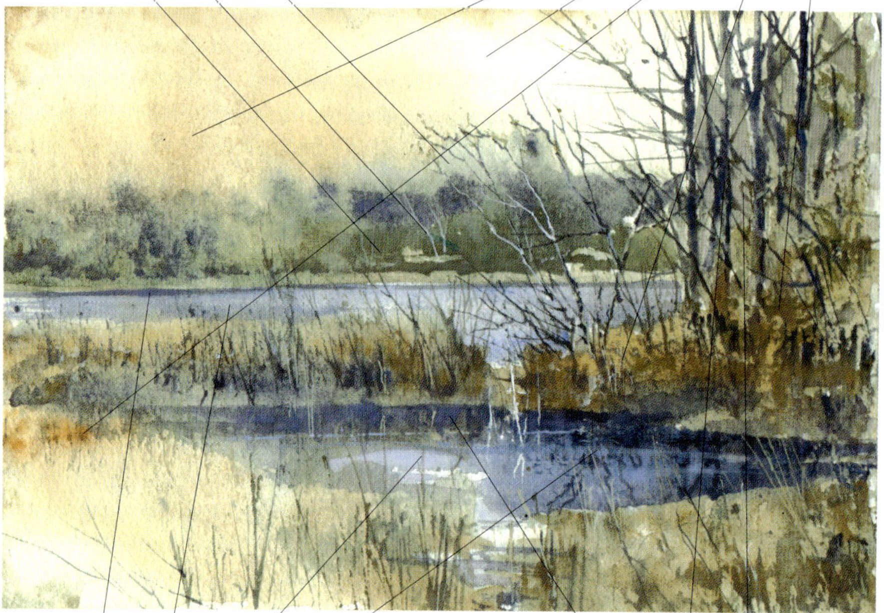

3a 8c 9c 9b
Cerulean Blue and
Phthalocyanine Blue
P50

2a 3 5c
Phthalocyanine Blue
and
Burnt Sienna P47

Pond water

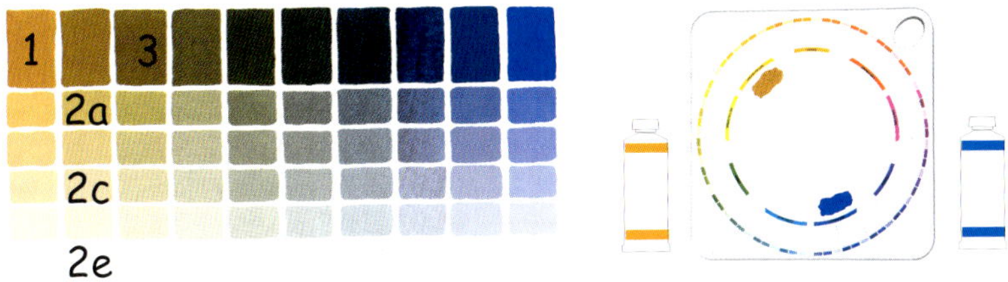

Raw Sienna and Ultramarine Blue P19

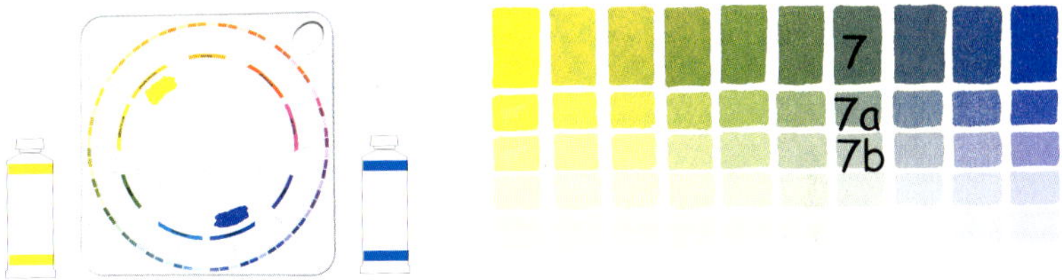

Cadmium Yellow Light and Ultramarine Blue P12

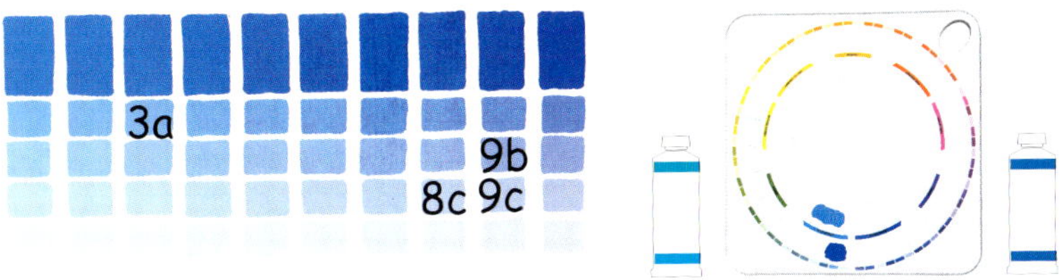

Cerulean Blue and Phthalocyanine Blue P50

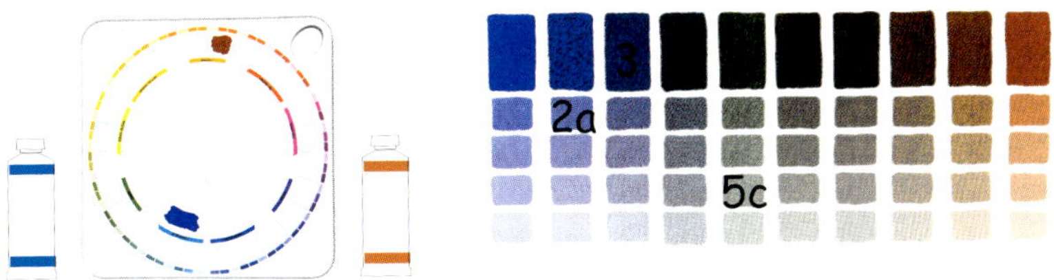

Phthalocyanine Blue and Burnt Sienna P47

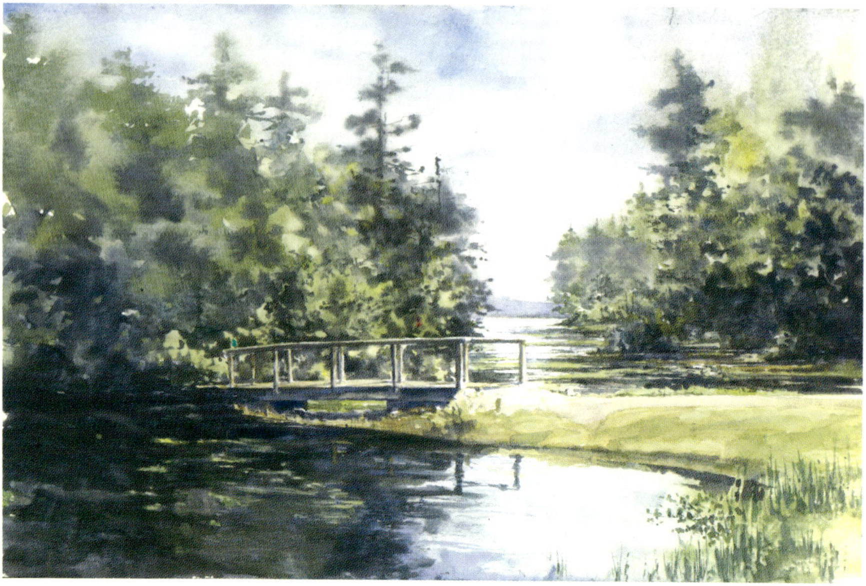

I often associate water with summer walks. The effect of sunlight on water is continually surprising and is often dramatic. In this painting I wanted to show a bright but hazy scene with high contrast yet some soft edges. I began with thin wet washes to the sky and lake of Cerulean Blue and Phthalocyanine Blue. I then immediately painted in the trees using Cadmium Yellow Light and Ultramarine Blue, allowing them to blend into the sky in places. The grasses were also painted with this mixture biased towards yellow. For darker greens, Phthalocyanine Green and Quinacridone Violet were used. Notice how all mixes are in keeping with the high contrast theme in the painting

Cerulean Blue and Phthalocyanine Blue P50

9a 9c 4e

Cadmium Yellow Light and Ultramarine Blue P12

8 3a 3c 4b

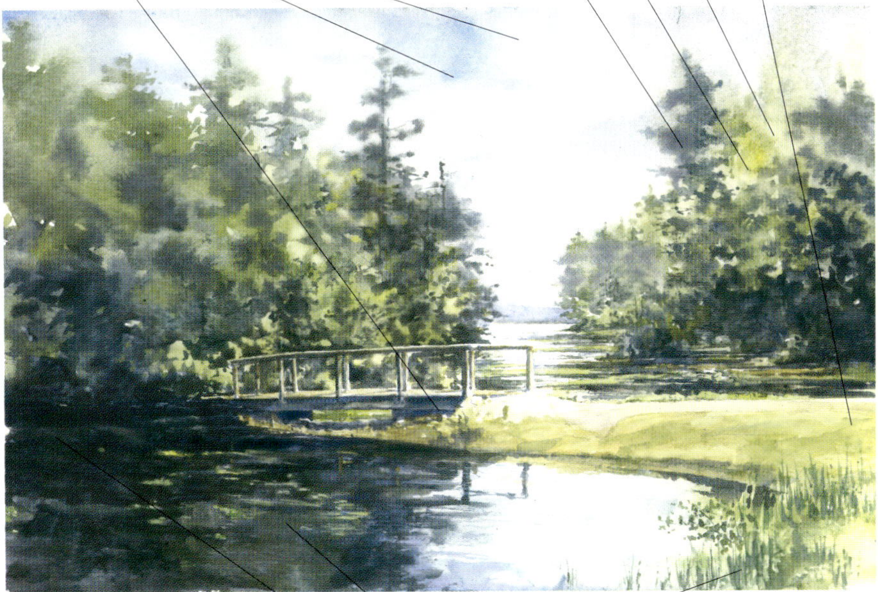

6 6a 7b

Phthalocyanine Green and Quinacridone Violet P21

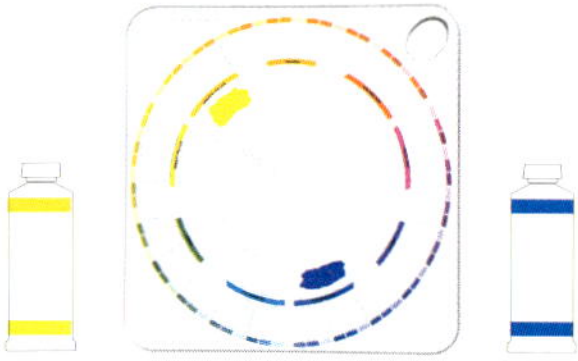

Page 12 of the Colour Mixing Swatch book.

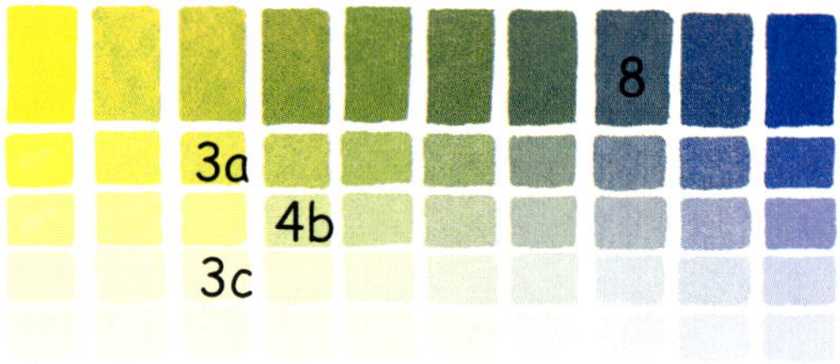

Cadmium Yellow Light and Ultramarine Blue

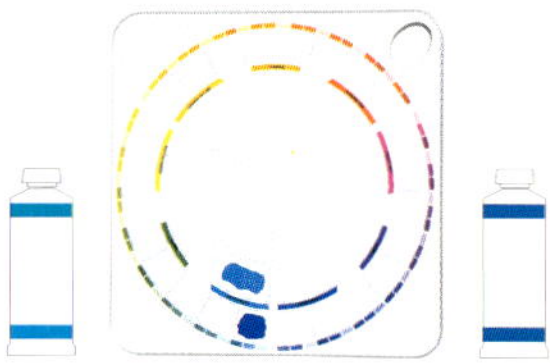

Page 50 of the Colour Mixing Swatch book.

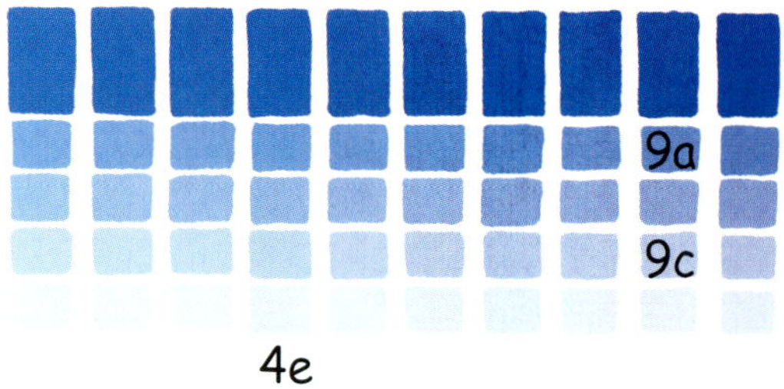

Cerulean Blue and Phthalocyanine Blue

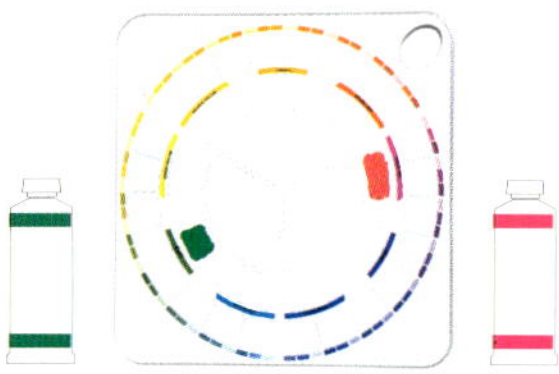

Page 21 of the Colour Mixing Swatch book.

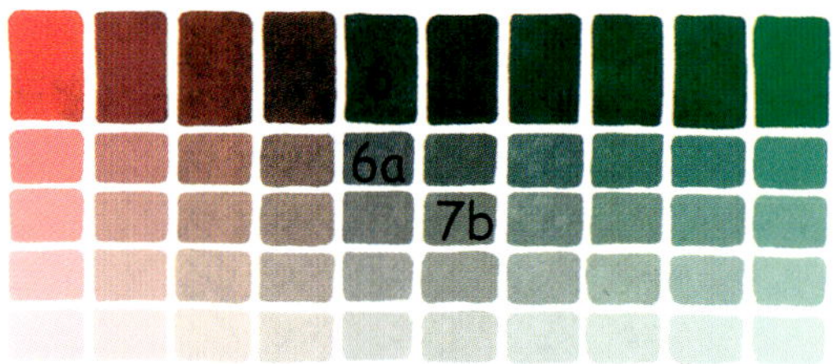

Phthalocyanine Green and Quinacridone Violet

Rushing water

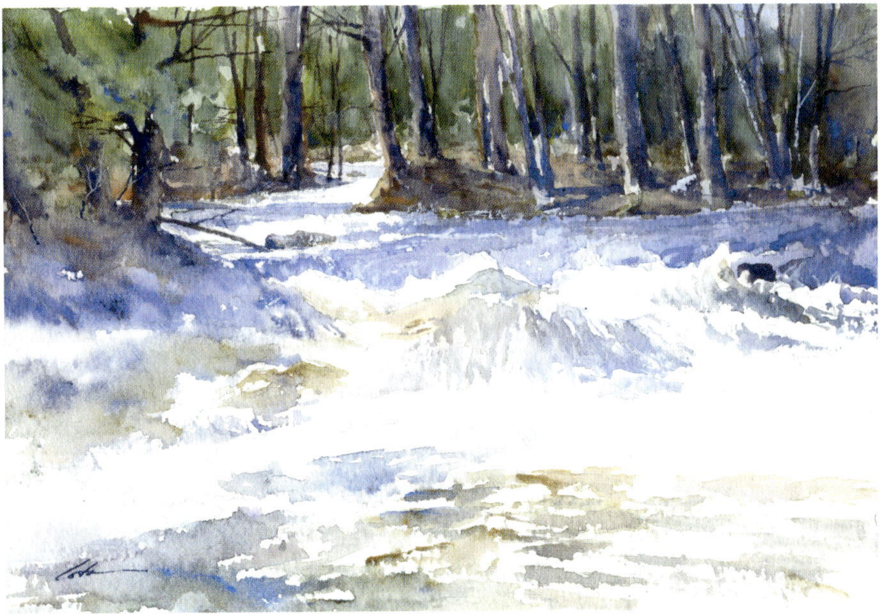

Capturing moving water is a challenge for artists of all abilities. I used colour to play an important role in depicting this movement. The distant water is 'cool' and subdued while the foreground water is bathed in 'warm' vibrant sunlight. This inbuilt tension helps to give the feeling of an ever-changing, ever-moving scene.

I was careful to leave plenty of white so that the strong contrast of the painting would remain.

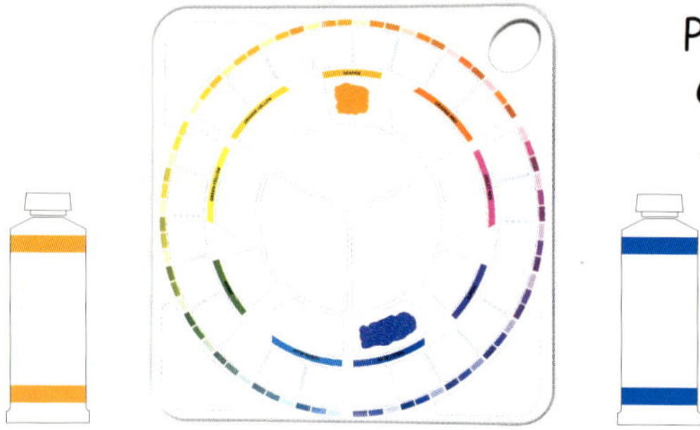

Page 48 of the Colour Mixing Swatch book.

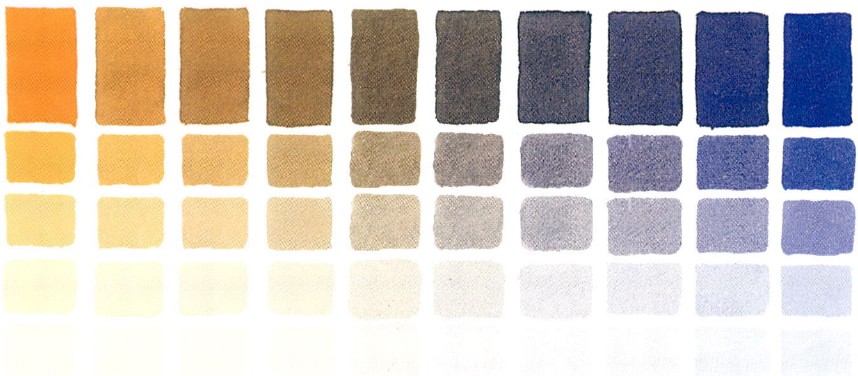

Much of the painting was produced from Ultramarine Blue and Burnt Sienna. This combination has an incredible range and can be extremely useful in many a painting. Being a complementary mixing pair (blue and orange) they will absorb each others light. As they are also both transparent the mixes become even darker around the centre of the range, giving dark 'coloured greys'. Such dark colours are invaluable when they can be produced to order.

Ultramarine and
Burnt Sienna P48

2a 7 5c 2c 3 3a 3d 9b 9c 9e 5d

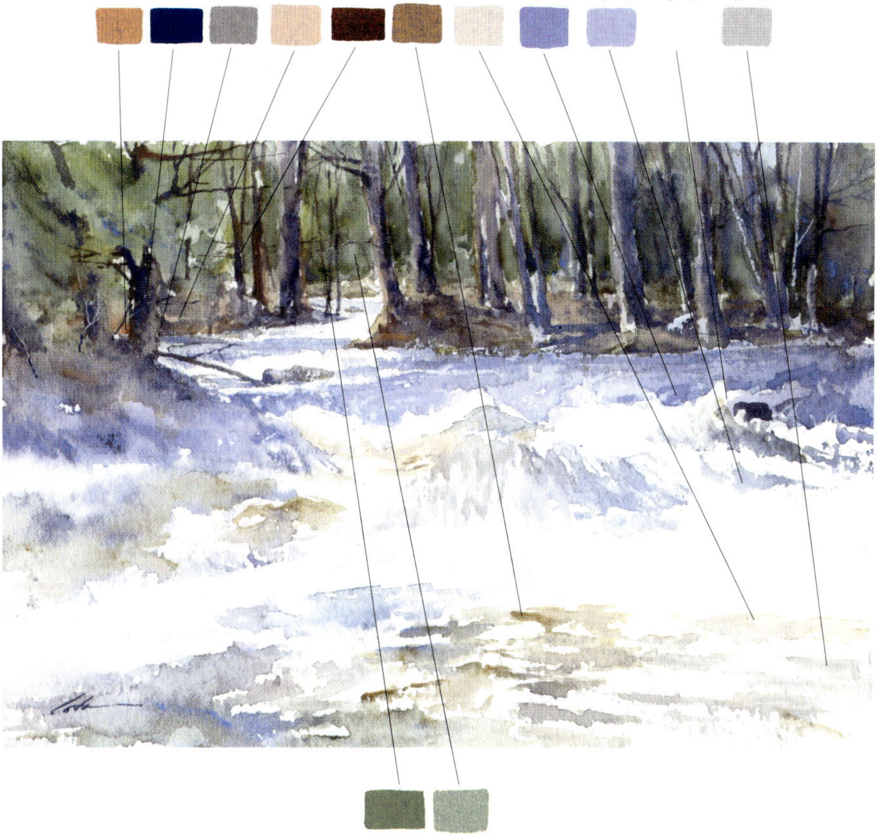

7 7a

Cad Yellow and
Ultramarine Blue P48

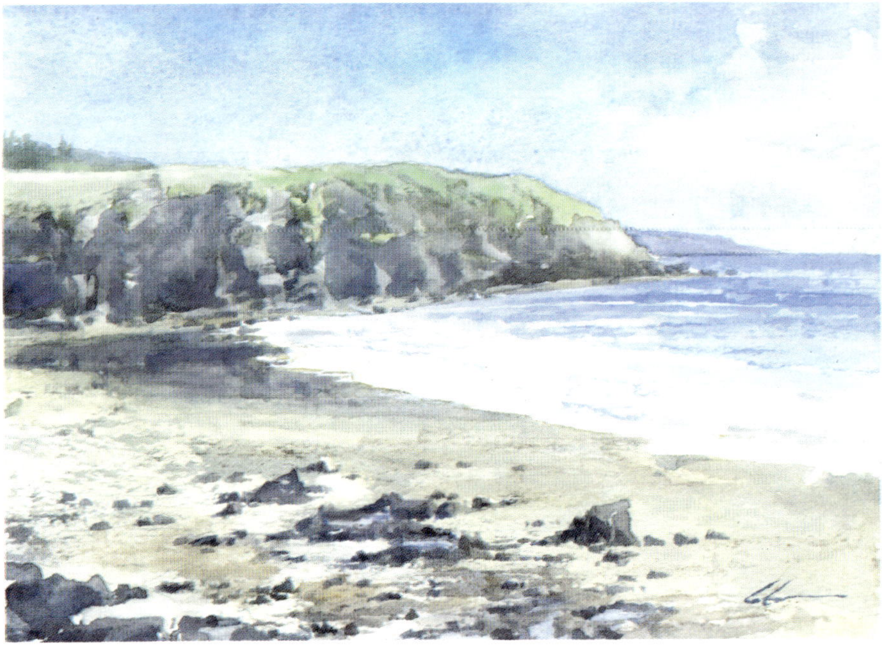

In this painting my aim was to work with a wide range of values to give the painting life. I started with a soft Cerulean Blue sky. This was applied in a loose wash which was carried into the water. When this wash was dry, Ultramarine Blue was added to the water in horizontal strokes making sure the darkest value would be the sea in the distance. The foam was simply the white of the paper, the lightest value. I painted the cliff tops with Cadmium Yellow Light and Cerulean Blue, with Cadmium Yellow Light being the most dominant. The cliff face and beach were painted with Ultramarine Blue and either Raw Sienna or Burnt Sienna, the latter being used where darker values were needed.

Burnt Sienna and
Ultramarine P48

7b 7d 7c 9b

Cadmium Yellow Light
and Cerulean P11

4b 10b 5b 10d

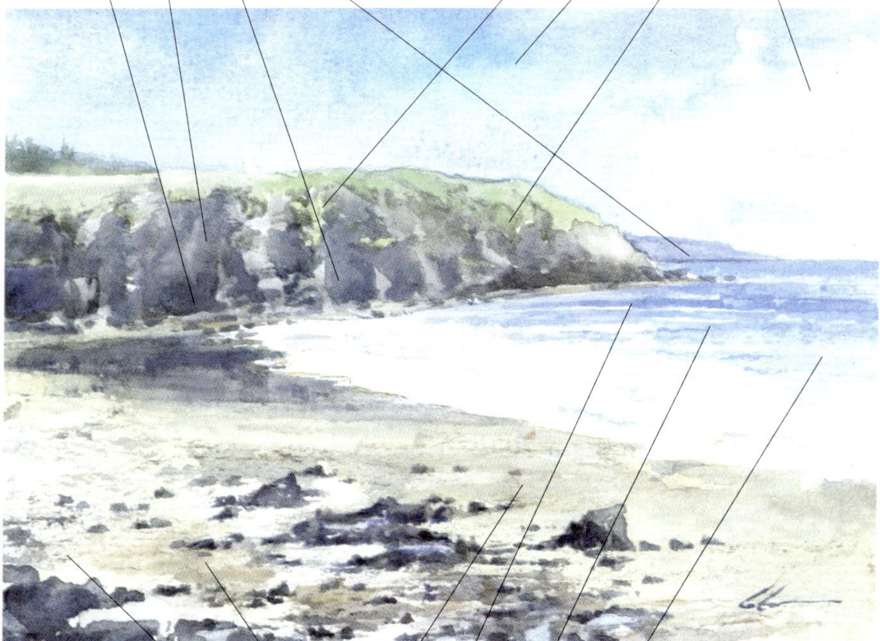

5e 4b 5d 10b 10c 10d

Raw Sienna and
Ultramarine P19

Deep reflections

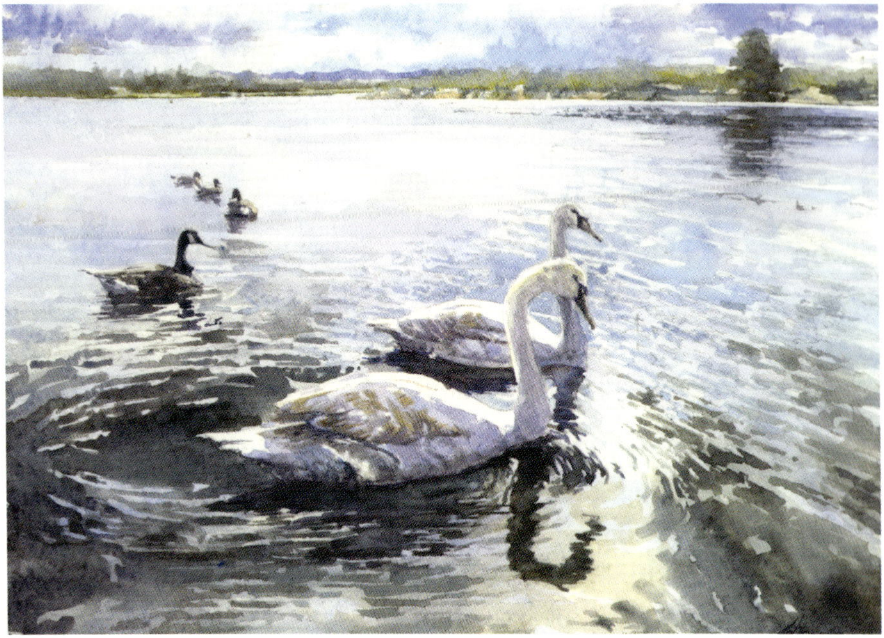

Often artists make the mistake of painting water 'all too blue'. Close observation tells us that water has a great number of values and colours to represent. In this painting, I wanted to paint a summer lake with strong deep contrasts yet still hold the delicate nature of the tranquil scene.
I began with the atmospheric sky of Cerulean Blue and Ultramarine Blue. These blends were also reflected in the water. A little Quinacridone Violet and Cerulean Blue gave delicate violet tints in places. Ultramarine Blue and Raw Sienna created the rich shadows as well as accents on the swans. Notice how the reflections remain dark despite the light colour of the swans they are reflecting.

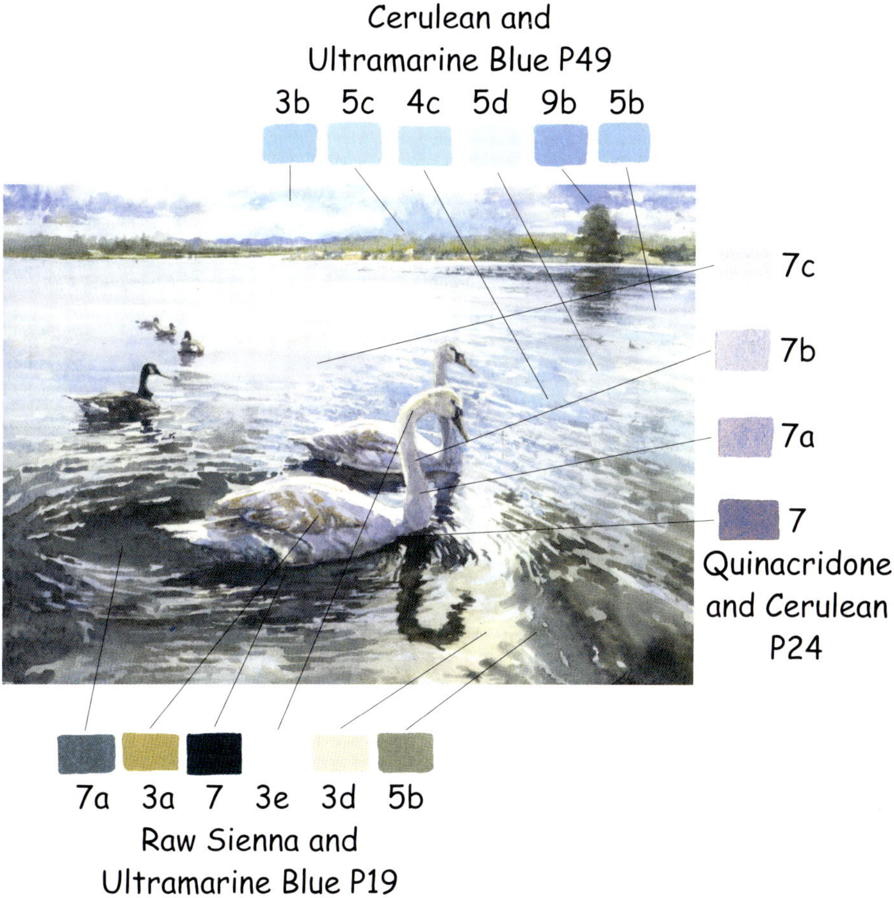
Cerulean and
Ultramarine Blue P49
3b 5c 4c 5d 9b 5b
7c
7b
7a
7
Quinacridone
and Cerulean
P24
7a 3a 7 3e 3d 5b
Raw Sienna and
Ultramarine Blue P19

Morning sea

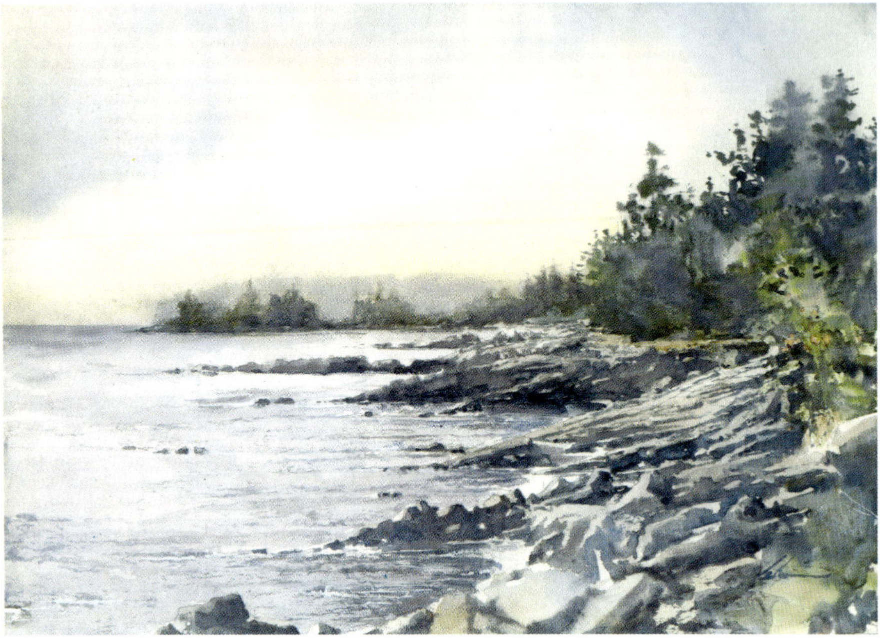

Although colour harmony is very much a matter of individual taste, one way to please the majority of viewers of your work is to use colours which are related to each other. Apart from the small areas of relatively bright green, the rest of the painting was produced from mixes of just two colours, Raw Sienna and Ultramarine Blue.

As nearly all of the colours used contain elements of these two hues they were relatively easy to harmonise. Artists tend very often to use too many colours in the one painting. This can lead to visual confusion rather than to colour harmony. The hue ranges from any of the swatches in the *Colour Mixing Swatch Book* can be used to this end.

Morning sea

Cad Yellow Light and
Ultramarine Blue P12

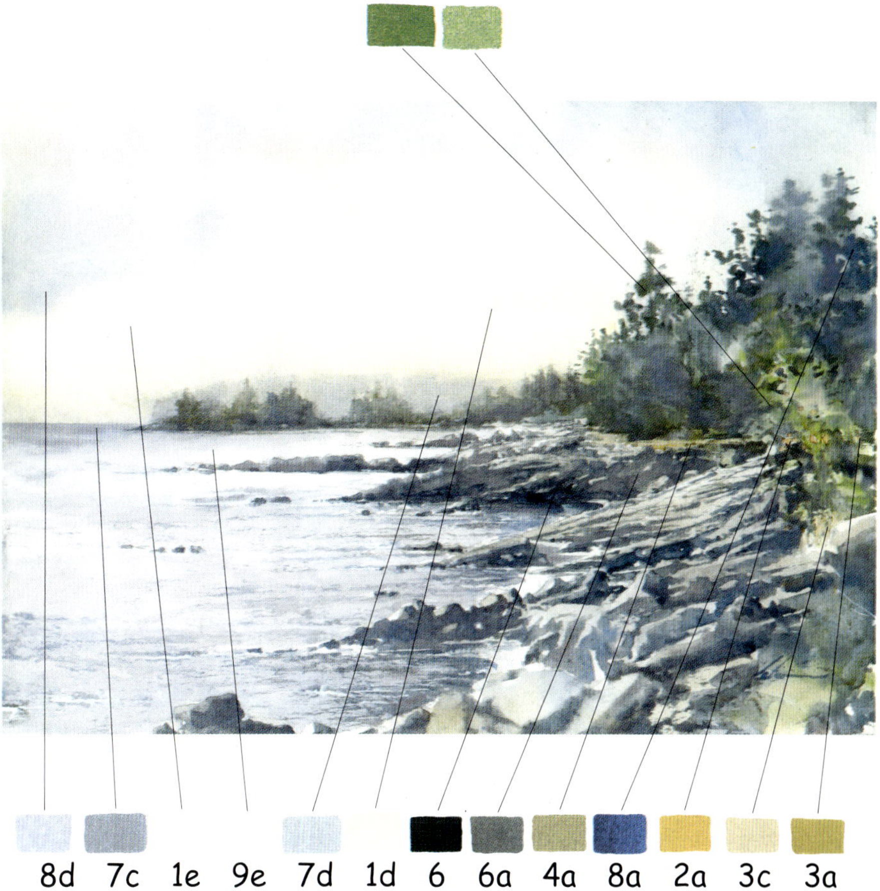

Raw Sienna and
Ultramarine Blue P19

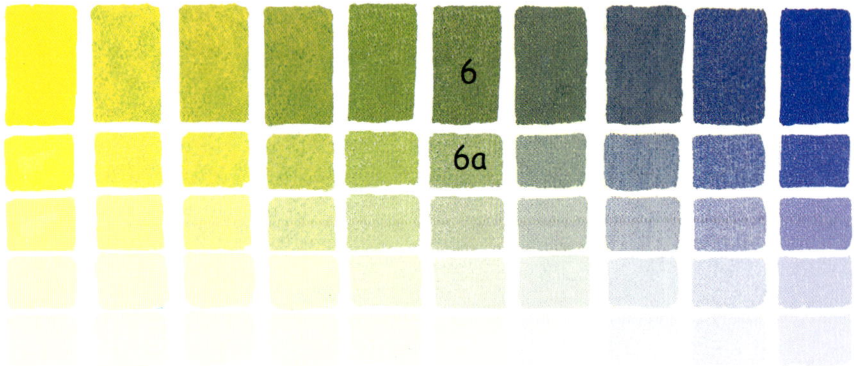

Cad Yellow Light and Ultramarine P12
These mixes were only introduced as such relatively bright greens cannot be produced from the main mixing partners, Raw Sienna and Ultramarine Blue.

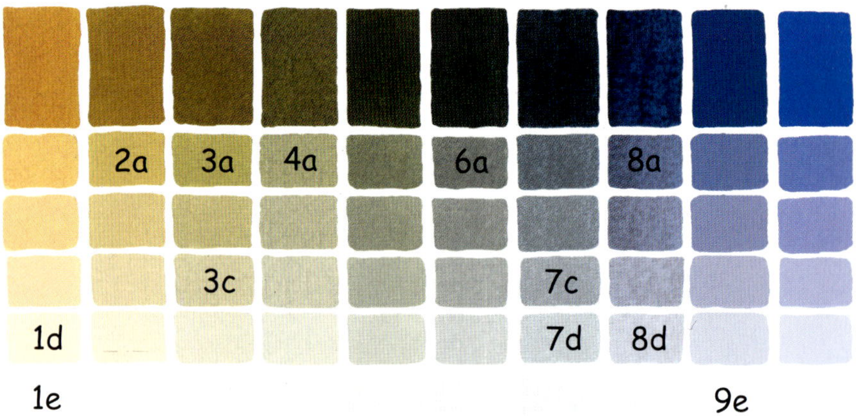

Raw Sienna and Ultramarine Blue P19. This valuable mixing pair give a wide range of hues, values and intensities.

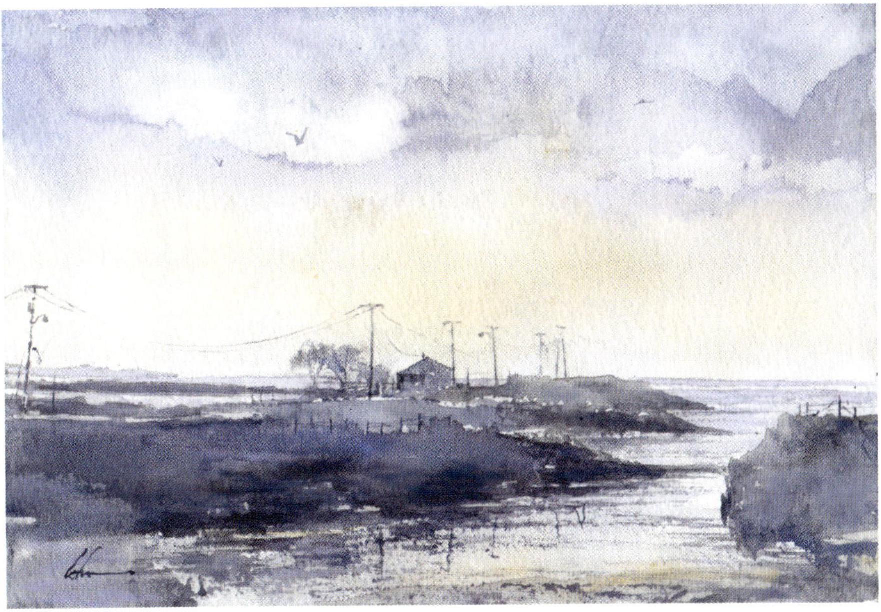

Water not only reflects the image of objects, but also the sky colour as well. This reflective property can set the tone of a painting. I used only three colours in this painting and aimed for a strong contrast. I began the piece by lightly applying Raw Sienna over the entire surface. Whilst this was still wet I laid a wash of Quinacridone Violet and Ultramarine Blue to the upper reaches of the sky. The surface was then allowed to dry thoroughly, after which a pale mix of Quinacridone Violet and Ultramarine Blue was used for the distant hills. Darker combinations of these two hues as well as Raw Sienna and Ultramarine Blue were used to paint the land masses.

Quinacridone Violet and
Ultramarine Blue P22

8b 8c 8e 8c 8

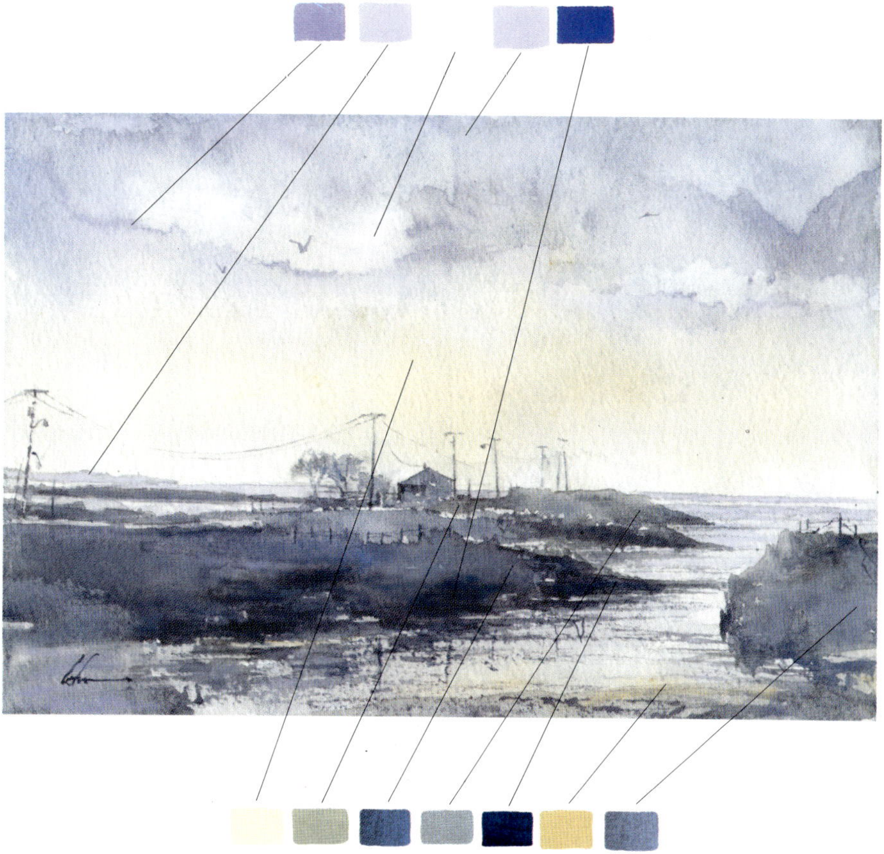

2d 5c 8a 7c 8 2b 8b

Raw Sienna and
Ultramarine Blue P19

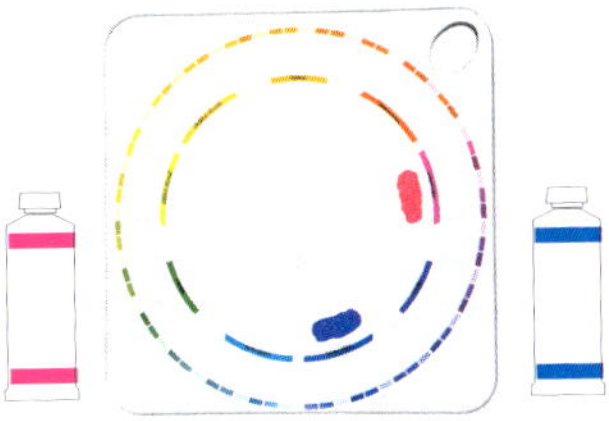

Page 22 of the Colour Mixing Swatch book.

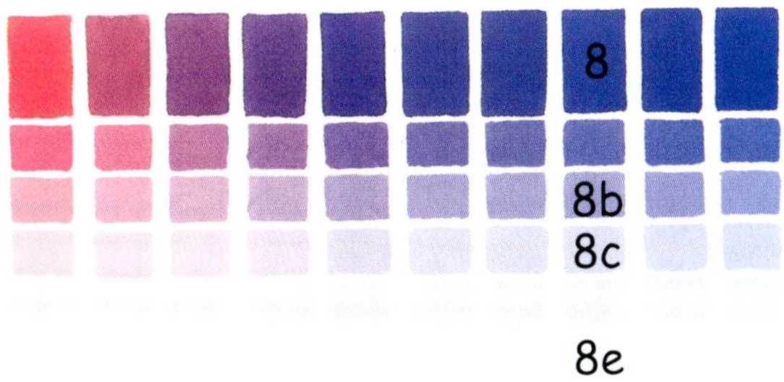

Quinacridone Violet and Ultramarine Blue

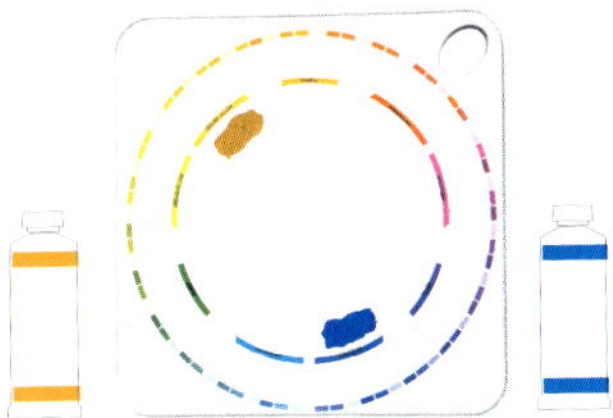

Page 19 of the Colour Mixing Swatch book.

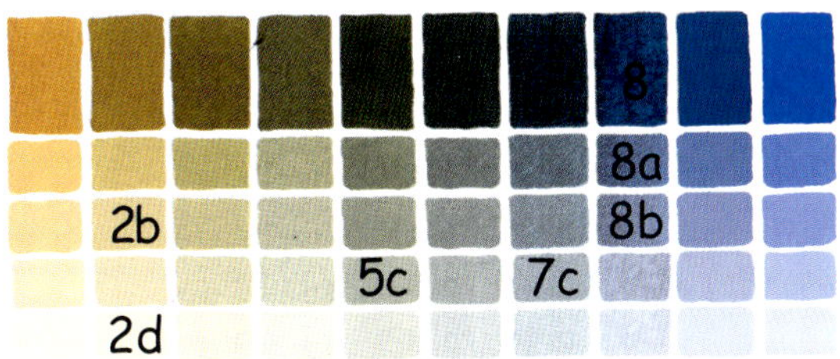

Raw Sienna and Ultramarine Blue

If you are seeking colour harmony, it often pays to use colours which are related to each other in some way. In this case the one blue has been used in both ranges. A credible painting could have been produced from Quinacridone Violet and Ultramarine Blue for the top range and Cerulean Blue and Burnt Sienna (page 46) for the lower. This approach would have removed the unity that using just one blue can help to bring about.

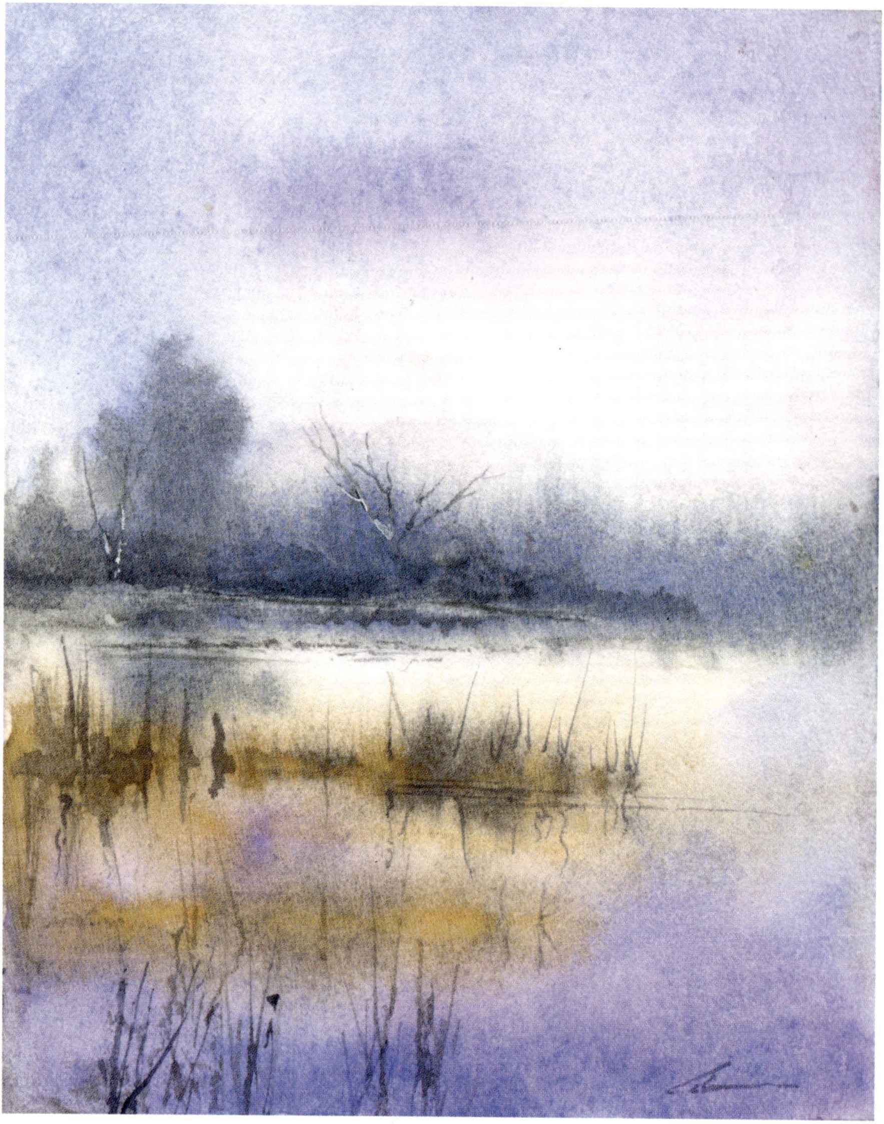

Misty water

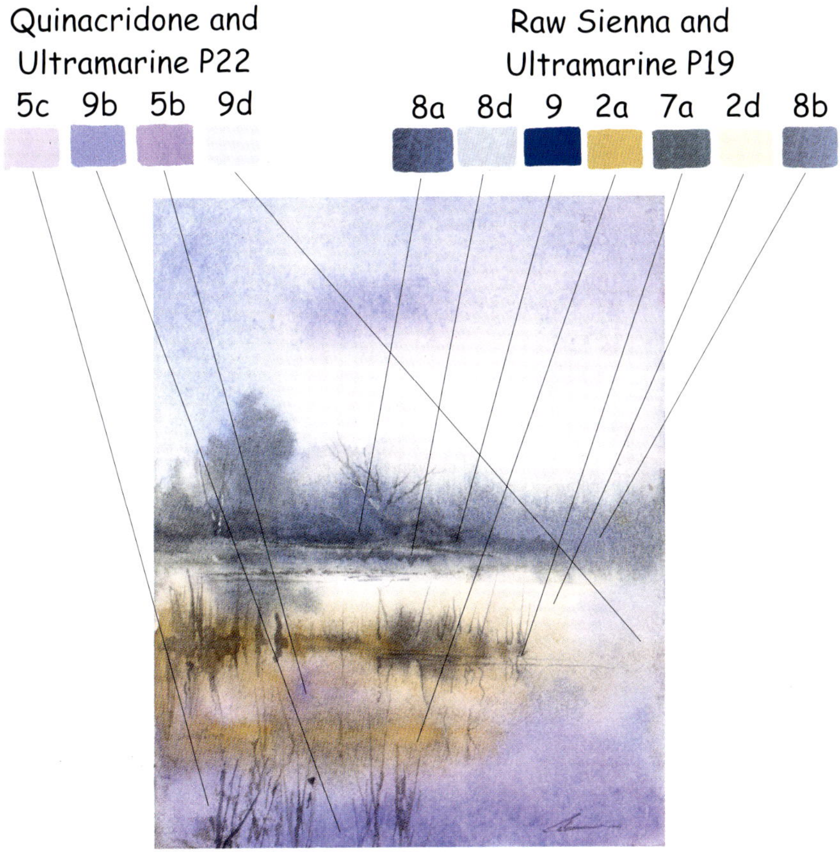

In this small study, I used just three colours to express the misty qualities of the scene. I began with a pale under painting of Raw Sienna and a tiny addition of Ultramarine Blue. This provided a 'warm' base for the painting. Whilst wet, Quinacridone Violet and Ultramarine were used to create the violets of the sky and water. Raw Sienna and Ultramarine was then painted in to suggest plants and other accents.

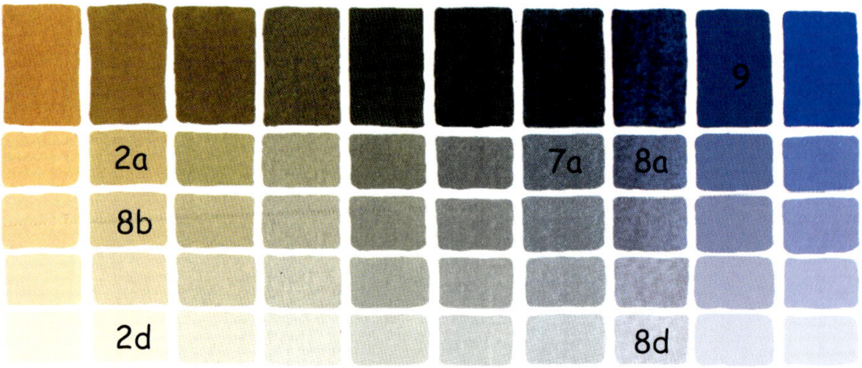

Raw Sienna and Ultramarine Blue P19

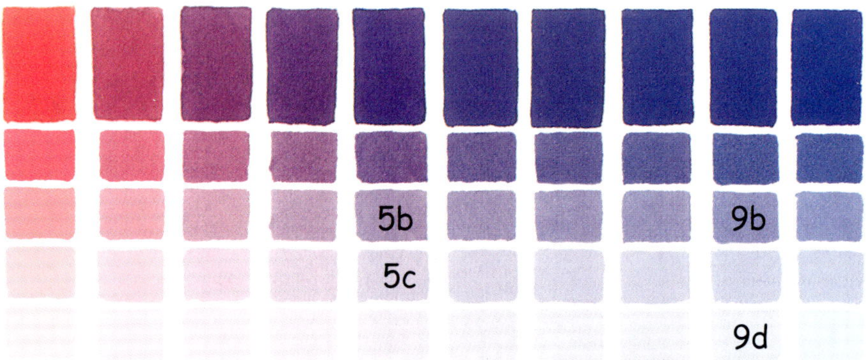

Quinacridone and Ultramarine Blue P22

Colour mixing and use can (and usually should), be kept simple and uncomplicated. In this case just three colours were put out on the palette, with most of the mixes simply applied at different strengths. Reduced either with water or with white paint.

Sunset

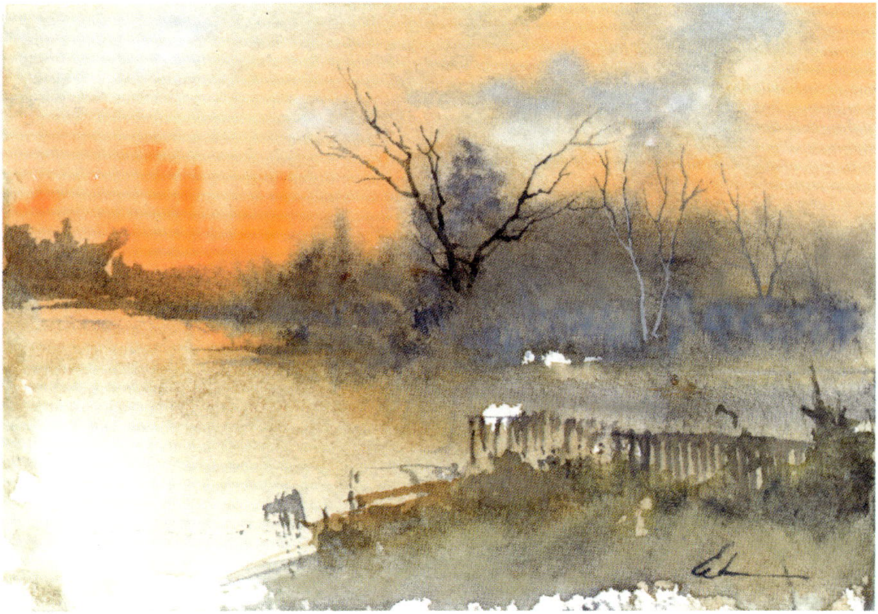

Little compares to the dramatic effect of sunset against water. Colours seem to become enhanced as they are repeated in reflection. I used just two colour combinations in this small study. I began with a mixture of Cadmium Red Light and Cadmium Yellow Light to form a bright orange. This orange was used for the 'saturated' areas in the sky. Cerulean Blue was added in varying amounts to create a wide range of dulled oranges and 'coloured greys'. The blue was also dulled by the orange to give the neutralised blues of the sky. I kept the water a lighter value overall. I finished off by adding accents to trees and fences using the same Cerulean Blue but changing its partner to Burnt Sienna.

Mixed Bright Orange and Cerulean Blue P44

1 6a 9d 9b 6 5 2c 2a

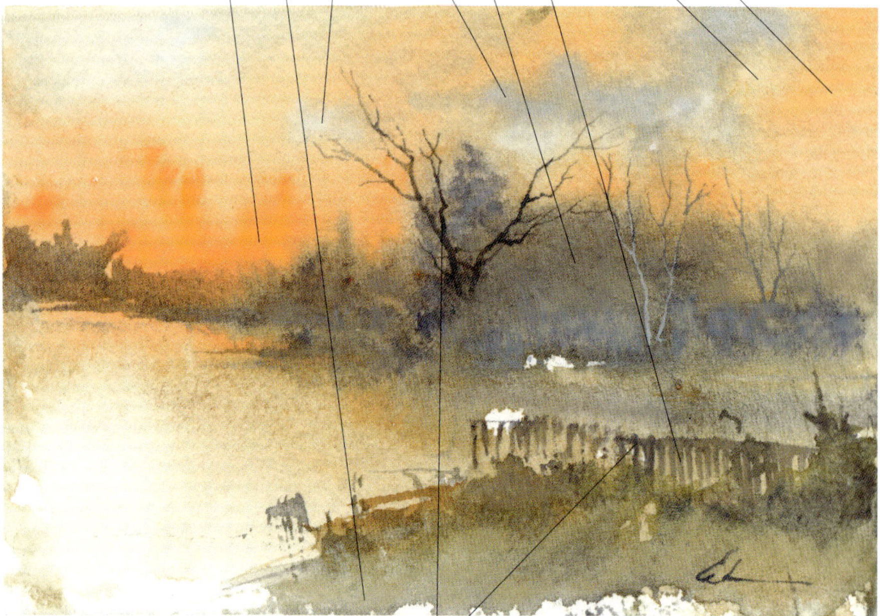

5

Burnt Sienna and
Cerulean Blue P46

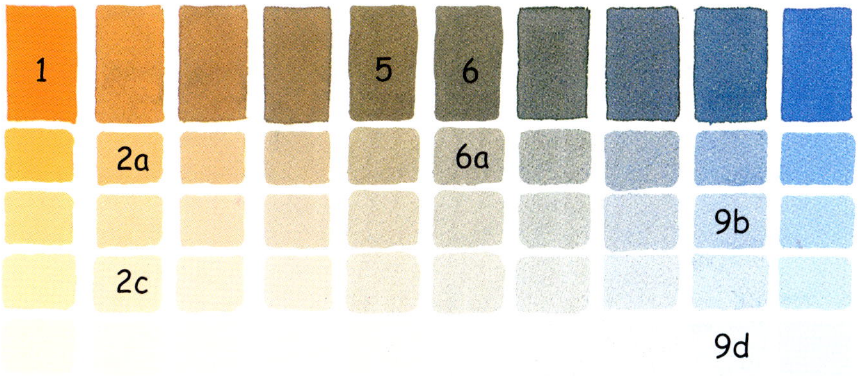

Mixed Bright Orange and Cerulean Blue P44

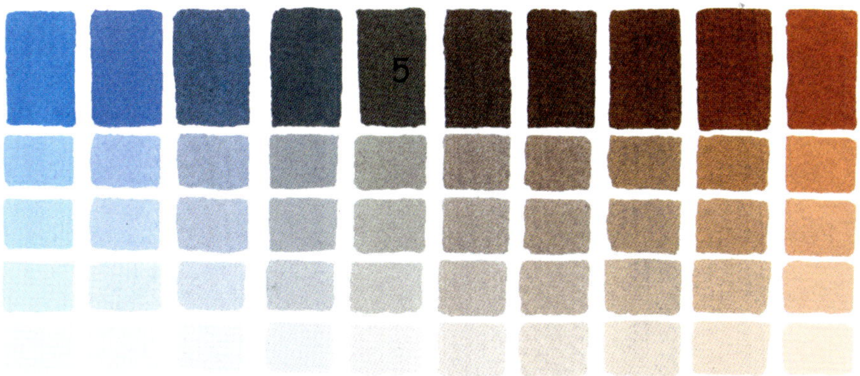

Burnt Sienna and Cerulean Blue P46

As a particularly dark 'brown' was required, the mixing partner to the blue was switched from a bright orange to the much darker and more transparent orange; Burnt Sienna.

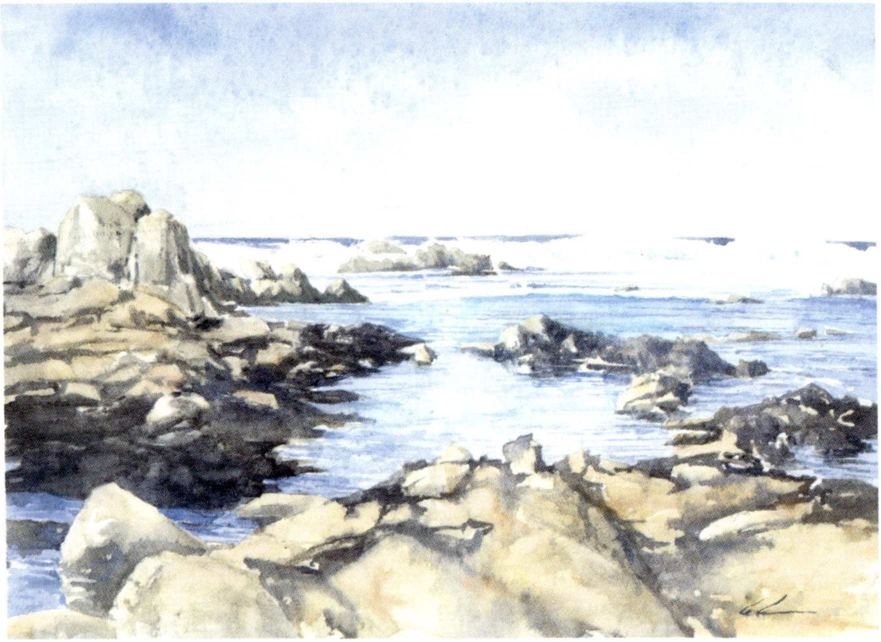

Sometimes the blue of the sea can be the true feature of a painting. This is particularly evident when placed next to complementary orange rocks. In this painting I wanted to create the bright blue sea often seen on holiday.
I used the intense Phthalocyanine Blue mixed with Ultramarine Blue to create layers of vibrant water. The complementary rocks were painted with Mixed Bright Orange and Cerulean Blue. Burnt Sienna and Ultramarine Blue was used for the darker, wet rocks.

Phthalocyanine Blue and
Ultramarine Blue P51

8d 8c 8e 8a 2b 3d 3c

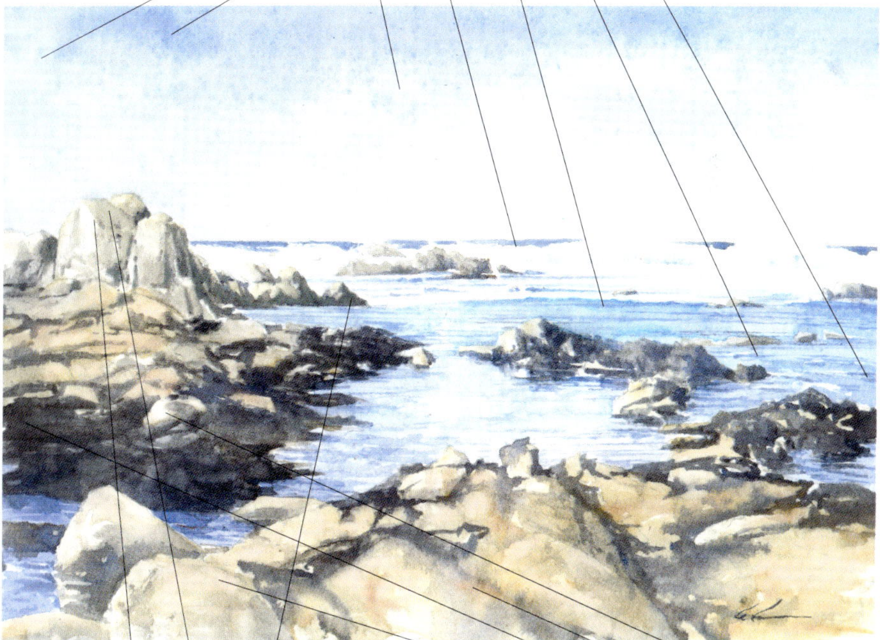

5e 6b 7
Mixed Orange
and Cerulean Blue P44

2d 6a 2c 2e
Burnt Sienna and
Ultramarine Blue P48

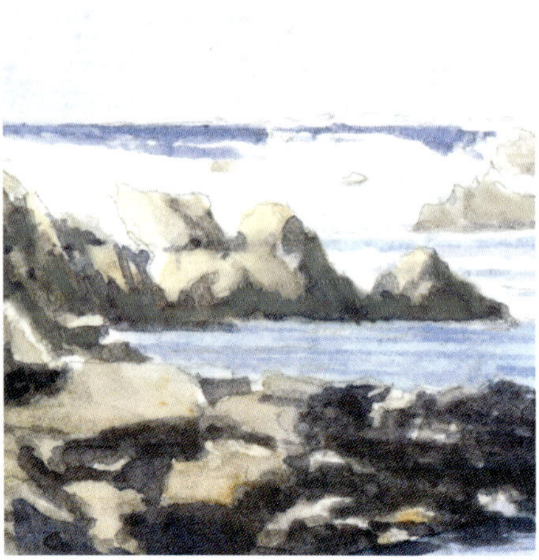

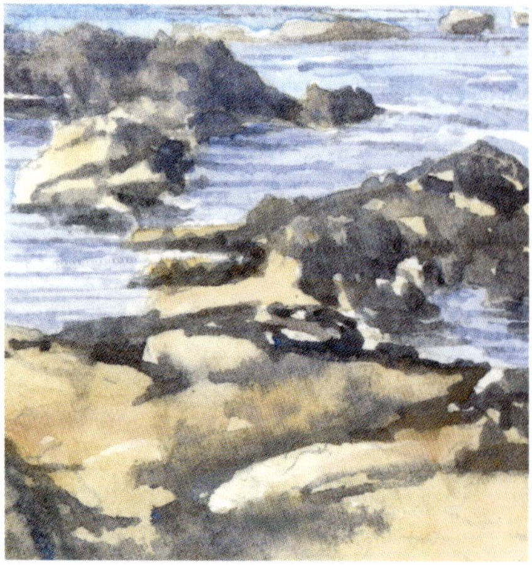

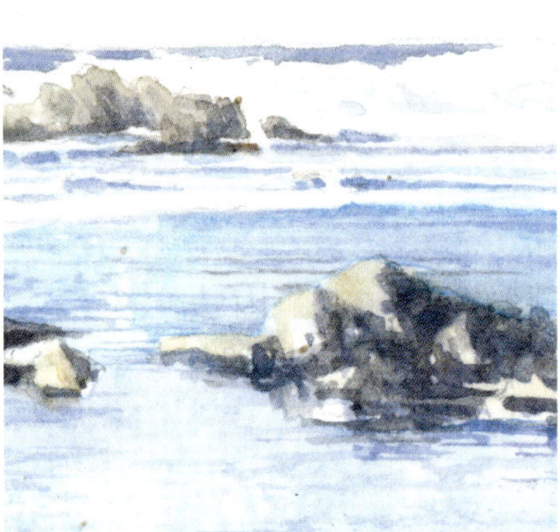

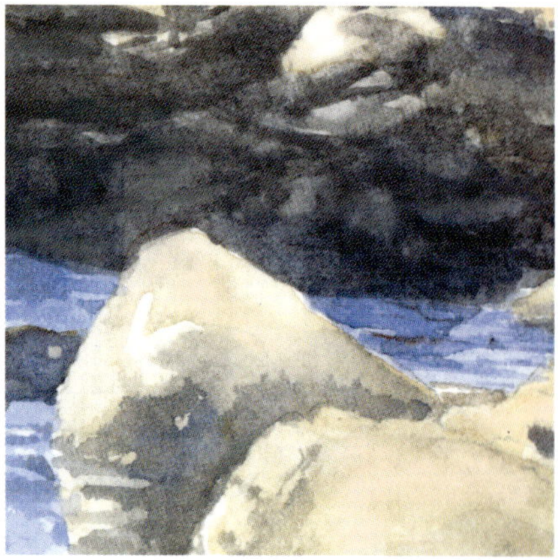

A complementary pair, such as blue and orange, will enhance each other visually when placed side by side or intermingled. That they are also mixing partners and will reduce each others intensity, as well as providing 'coloured greys' is an added bonus. The use of complementary pairings was central to the approach taken by the Impressionists.

Mediterranean sea

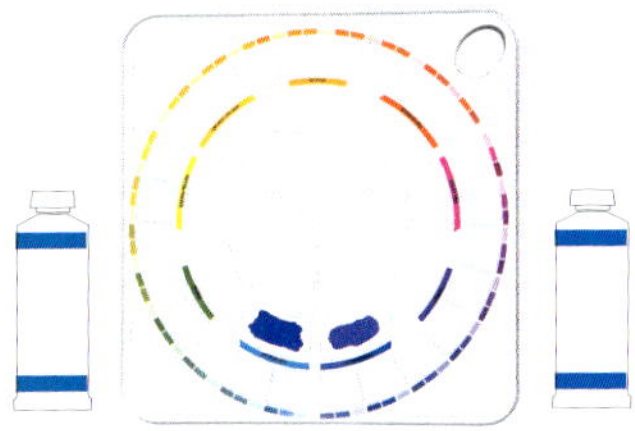

Page 51 of the Colour Mixing Swatch book.

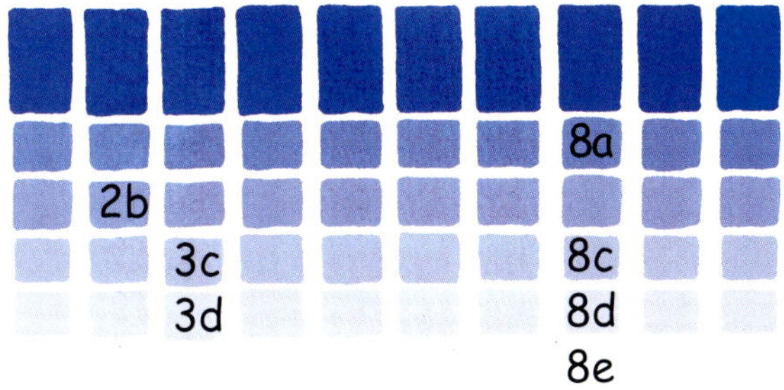

Phthalocyanine Blue and Ultramarine Blue

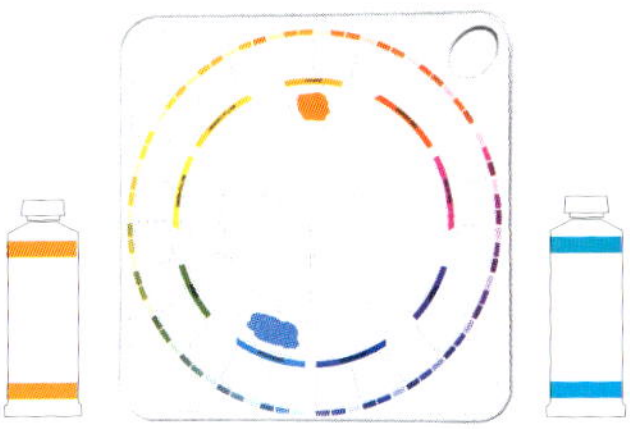

Page 44 of the Colour Mixing Swatch book.

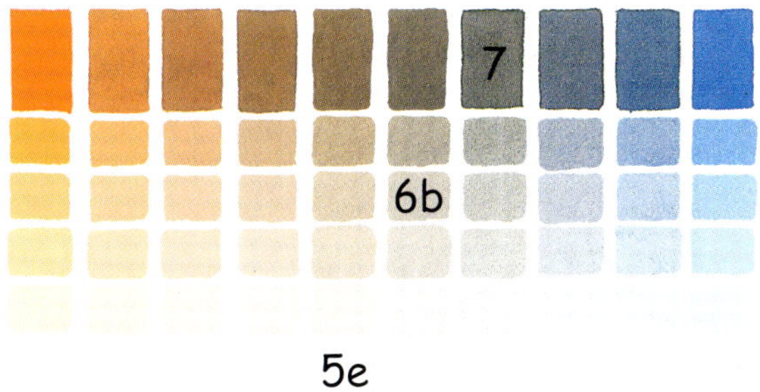

Mixed Orange and Cerulean Blue

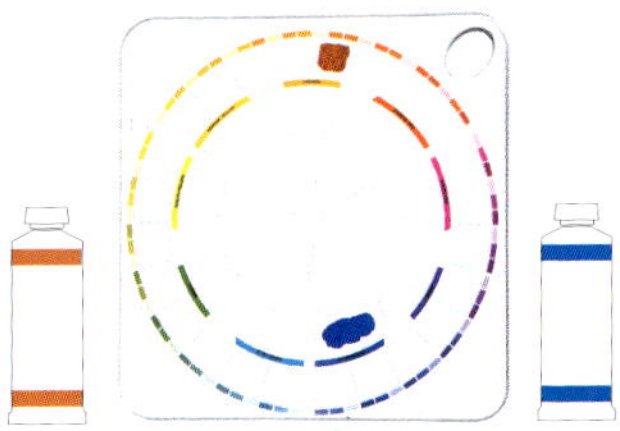

Page 48 of the Colour Mixing Swatch book.

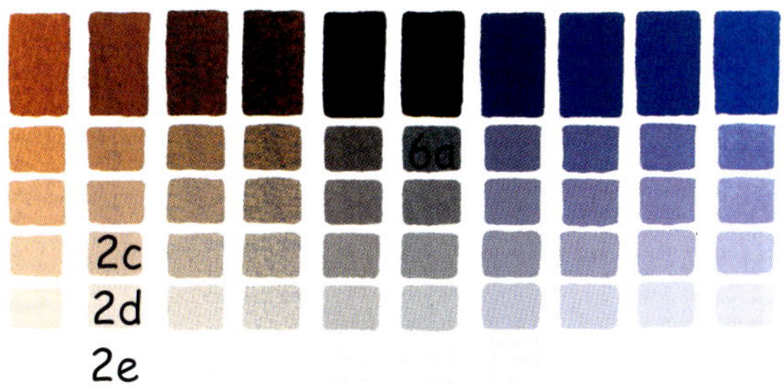

Burnt Sienna and Ultramarine Blue

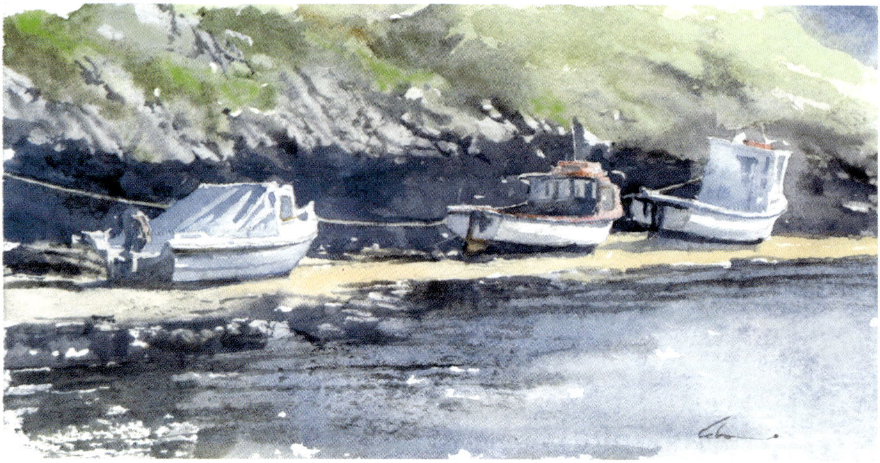

In this painting the high contrast of the water implies the reflection of a bright sky, only a glimpse of which has been shown. That versatile pair, Mixed Bright Orange and Cerulean Blue gave a range which extended from the light shore line to the various 'coloured greys' in the rocks. They also provided much of the colour in the water, and boats. The latter were finished with 'touches' of Cadmium Red Light to complement the background greens.

The greenery was painted with various mixes of Hansa Yellow and Ultramarine Blue, a mixing pair which give useful mid-intensity greens. The darks produced from Ultramarine Blue and Burnt Sienna, another very versatile combination, gave a strong light/dark contrast in the rocks and water.

By sandwiching the pale orange between two areas of blue, use has been made of the fact that they are a complementary pair, and will enhance each other visually.

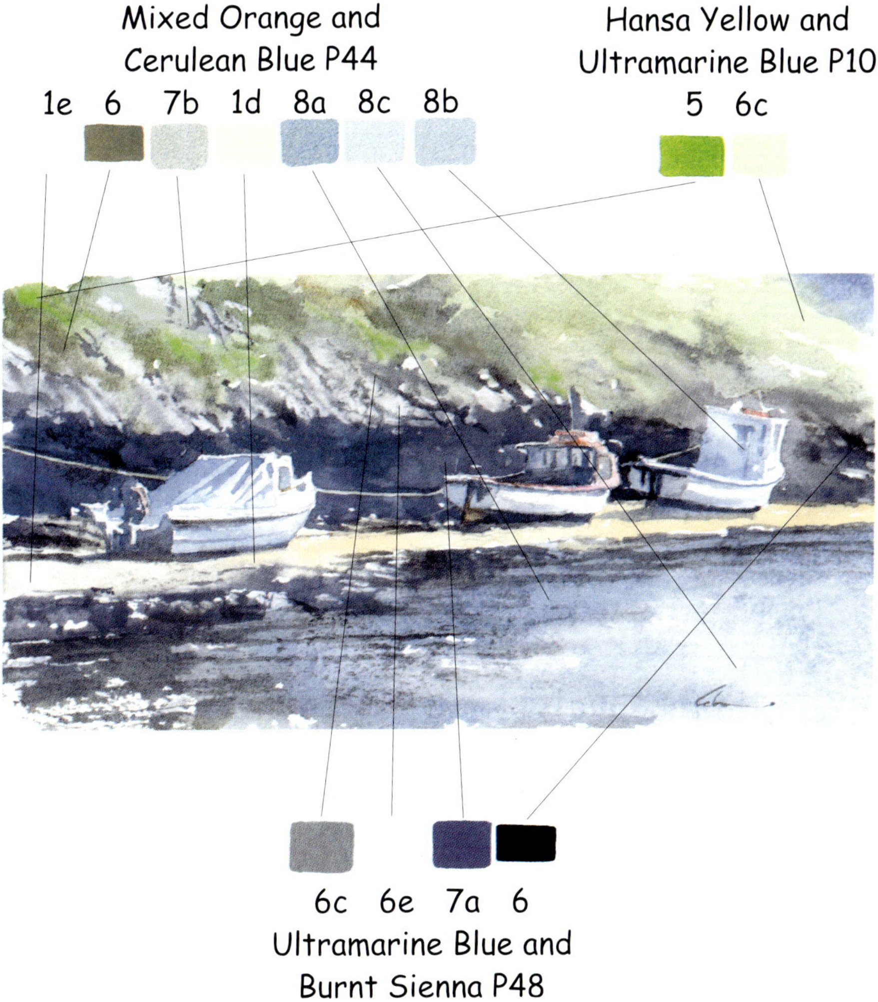
Mixed Orange and
Cerulean Blue P44
1e 6 7b 1d 8a 8c 8b
Hansa Yellow and
Ultramarine Blue P10
5 6c
6c 6e 7a 6
Ultramarine Blue and
Burnt Sienna P48

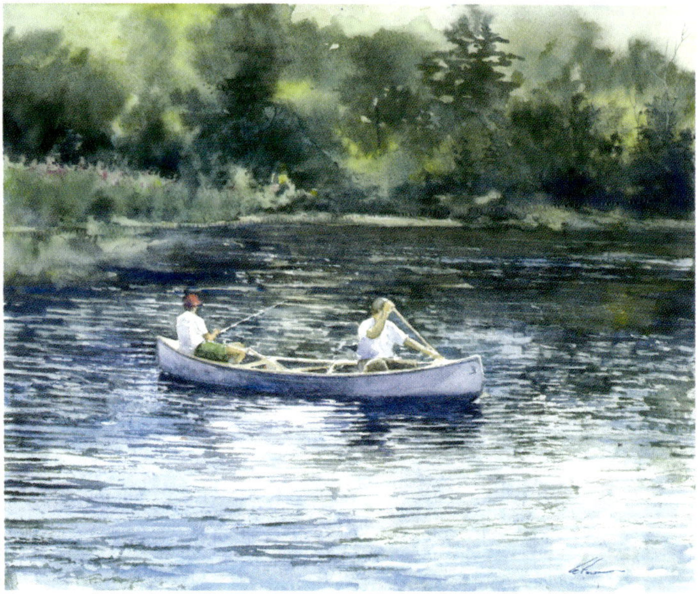

I find it better to paint moving water in layers. I used Cerulean Blue modified with a little Titanium White for the initial pale wash of the water and sky. The white muted the mixture, allowing the wash 'body colour' but with reduced intensity. The darker mixes were applied after the initial wash had dried. This ensured that the edges of the brush strokes were sharp. This would not have been the case had the initial wash been at all damp. Hansa Yellow and Cerulean Blue, which give a range of bright greens, were used in the background trees. Darker greens were mixed from Quinacridone Violet and Phthalocyanine Green. This combination provided some of the darks in the water as well.

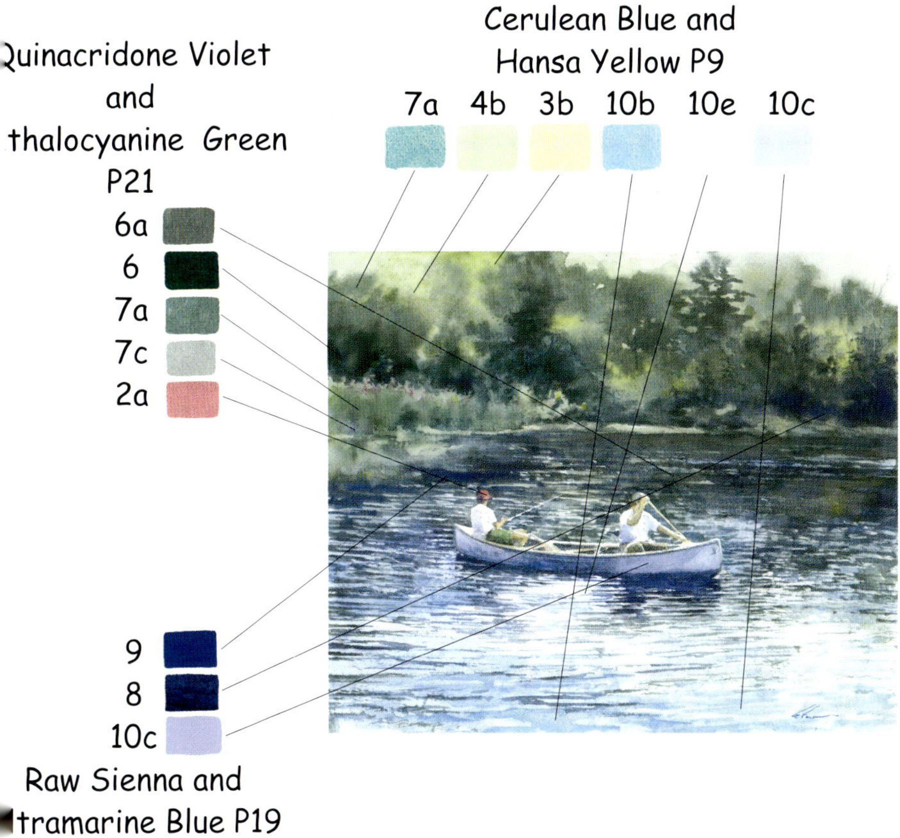

The figures were then painted, ensuring they stayed light against the background. The skin tones came from Raw Sienna and Ultramarine, Quinacridone Violet with a touch of Phthalocyanine Green was used for the hat. This red/green combination is very versatile. Both hues are transparent and very intense. In mixes they will neutralise or dull each other as well as give some wonderful darks.

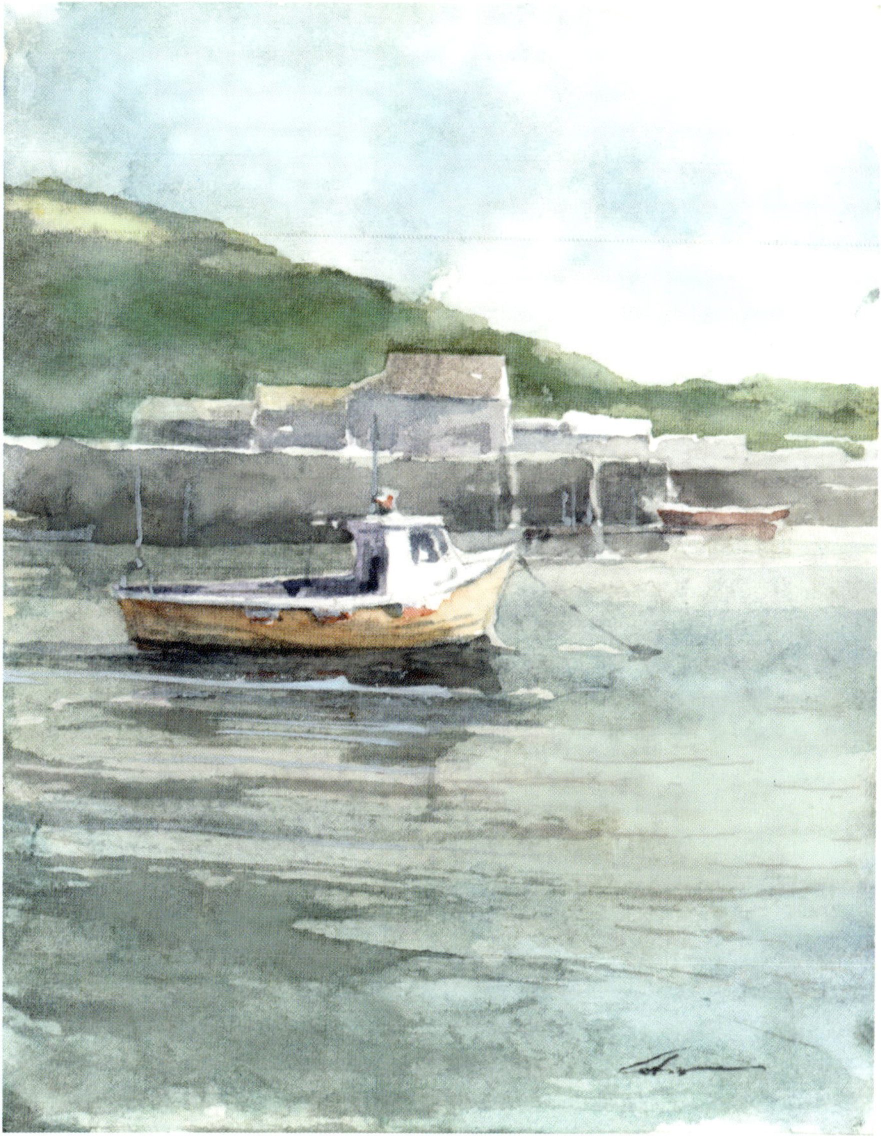

Shallow harbour water

In this scene, the shallow water allowed sunlight to pass through the surface and reflect from the green algae covered floor of the harbour. This influence can vary the colour of the water from a murky 'near black' to a vibrant rich green. I often use Phthalocyanine Green in this sort of application as it has a wonderful 'marine' quality. If used and mixed carefully it can bring interest to what could easily be dull, lifeless water.

I began this painting with a wash of Phthalocyanine Green and Cerulean Blue to the water. I was careful to keep a wide range of values with the lightest towards the brighter background. When the sky was dry, the background hills were painted with Hansa Yellow and Phthalocyanine Blue. This valuable mixing pair will give a wide range of very bright, transparent greens.

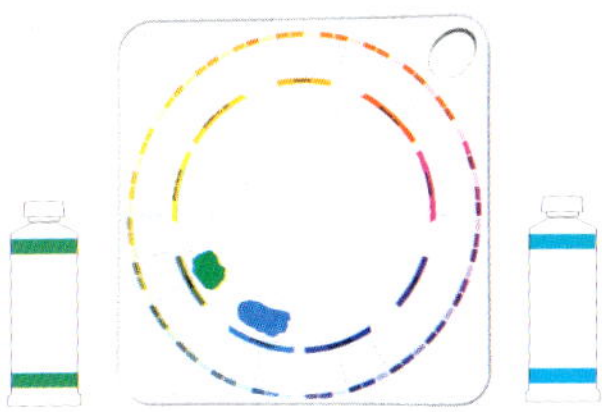

Page 16 of the Colour Mixing Swatch book.

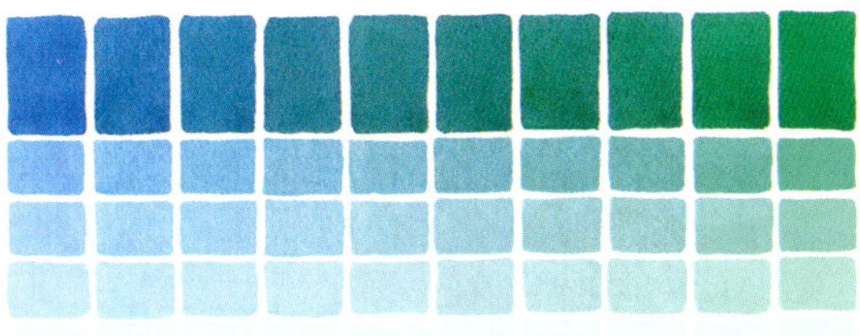

Phthalocyanine Green and Cerulean

As the Cerulean Blue is opaque and the Phthalocyanine Green transparent, expect a range which varies from semi opaque green blues to semi transparent blue greens.

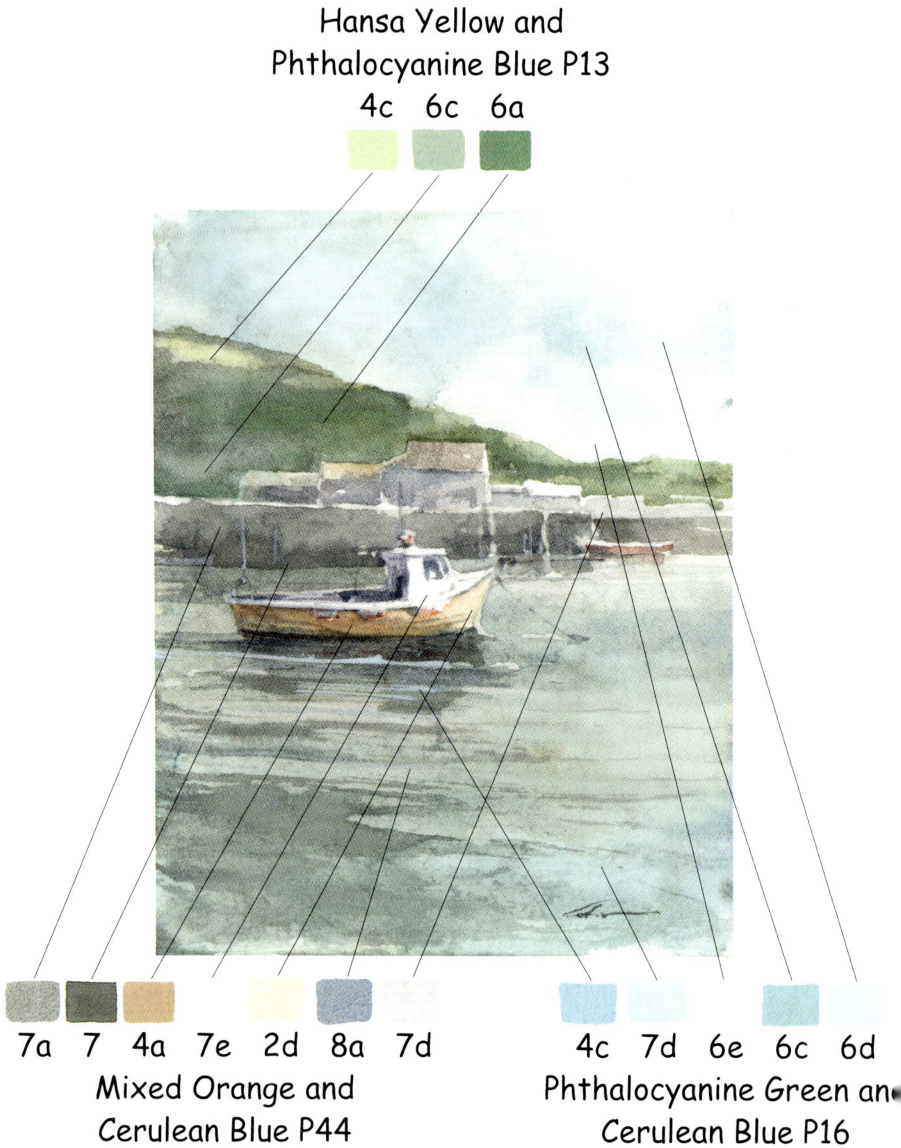
Hansa Yellow and
Phthalocyanine Blue P13
4c 6c 6a
7a 7 4a 7e 2d 8a 7d
Mixed Orange and
Cerulean Blue P44
4c 7d 6e 6c 6d
Phthalocyanine Green an
Cerulean Blue P16

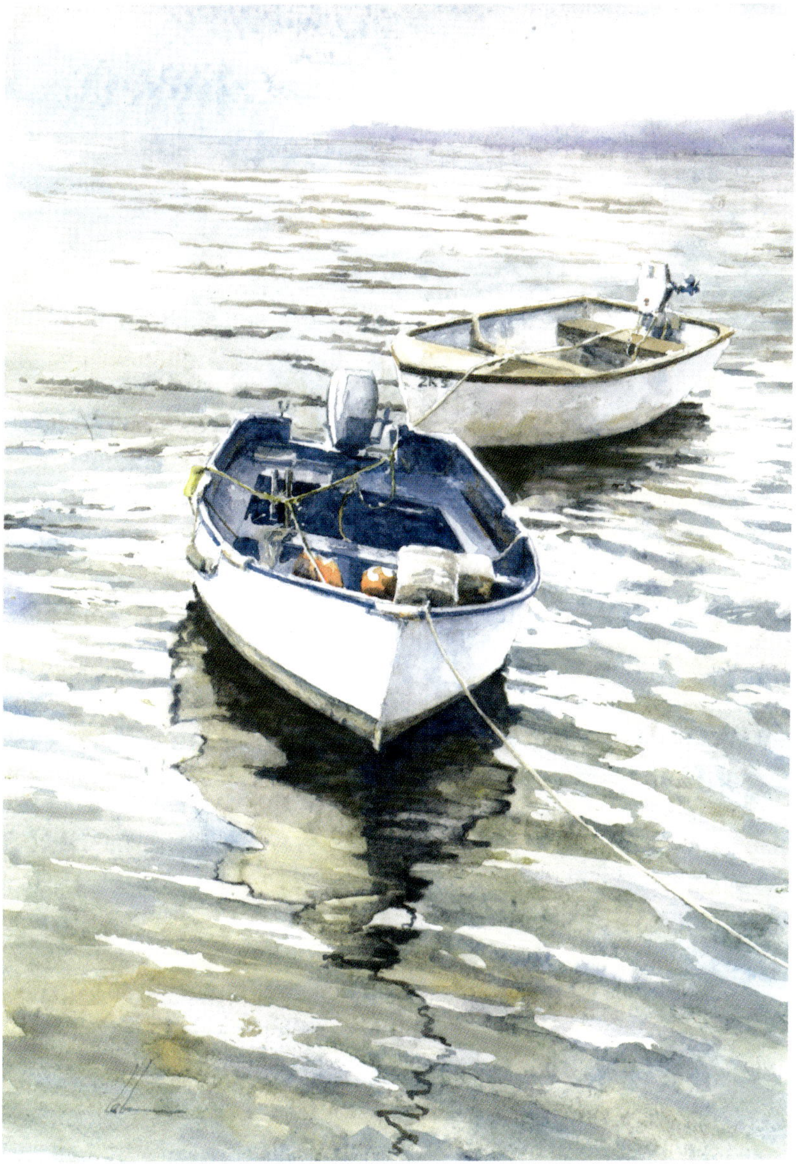

Boat reflections

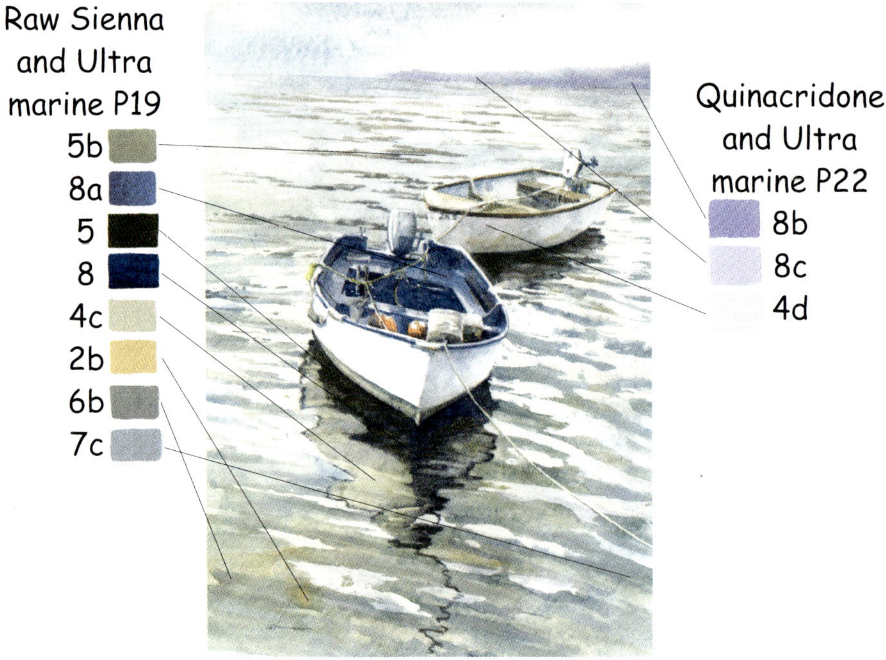

It is not easy to depict the reflections of objects in the water. The shifting planes cause constant value and colour change. Before commencing a piece such as this I often make several quick, rough colour studies, trying out different combinations.

In this painting one of the studies suggested that the range obtainable from Raw Sienna and Ultramarine Blue would work very well. You might find it useful to select a swatch from the *Colour Mixing Swatch Book* which looks as if it has potential for a particular scene. Apply the two colours to your palette and try out several of the mixes in a similar quick study. This can be valuable preparation.

Boat reflections

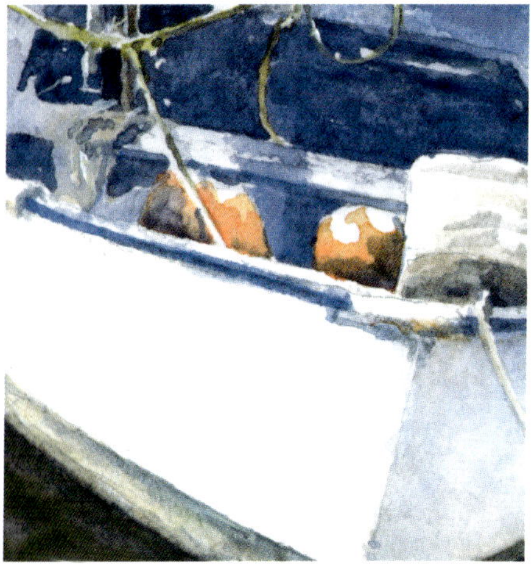

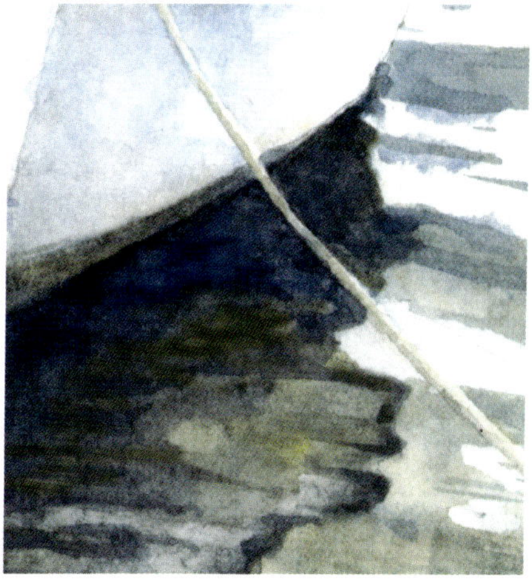

Apart from small touches of Cadmium Red Light, almost the entire painting was produced using just two colours. This approach can certainly be a great help if you are seeking harmony.

Where shadow interrupts the bright reflections of the sky it is possible to see beneath the surface of the water. For this reason, plus the effect of the shadow, such areas can appear very dark.

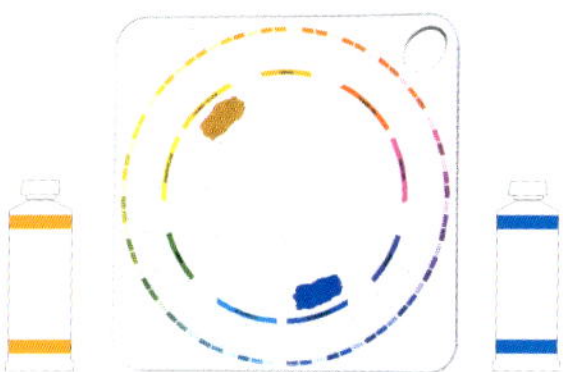

Page 19 of the Colour Mixing Swatch book.

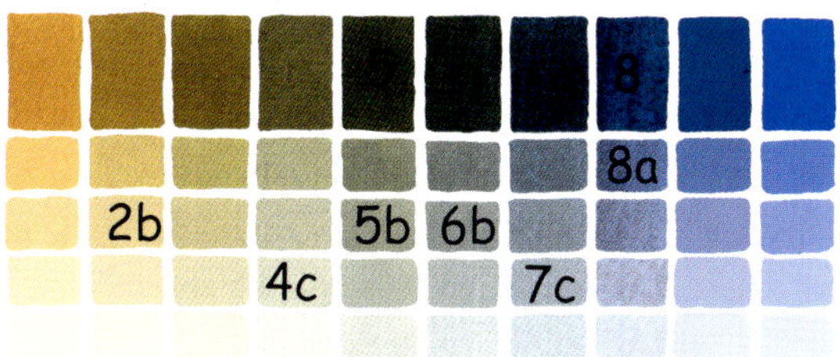

Raw Sienna and Ultramarine Blue

Other titles in the series

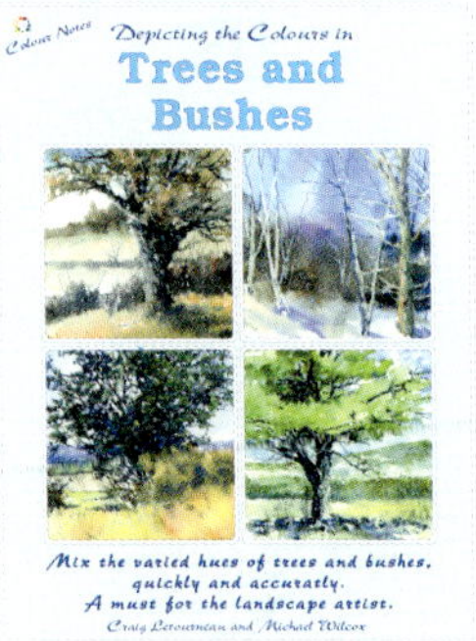

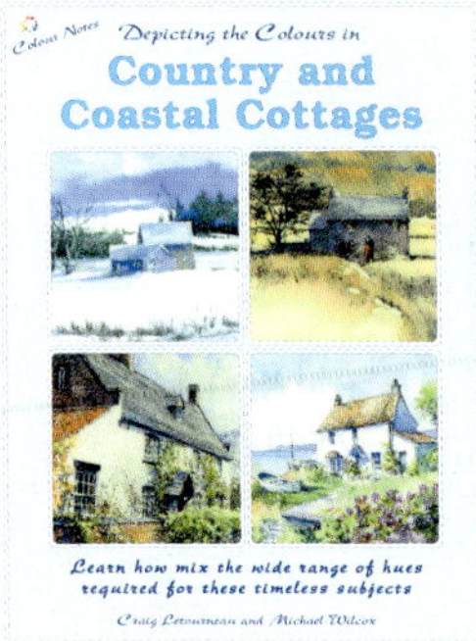

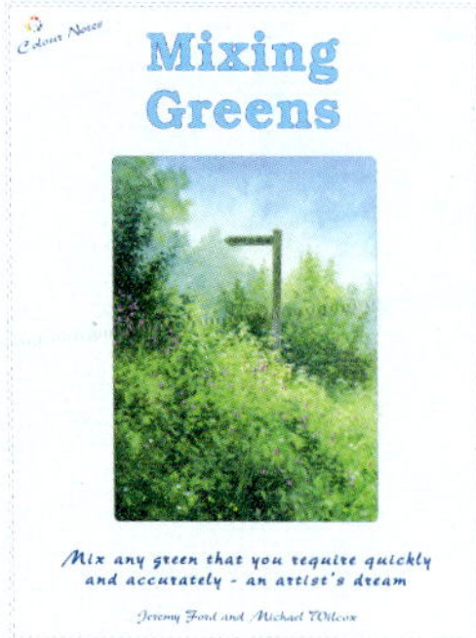

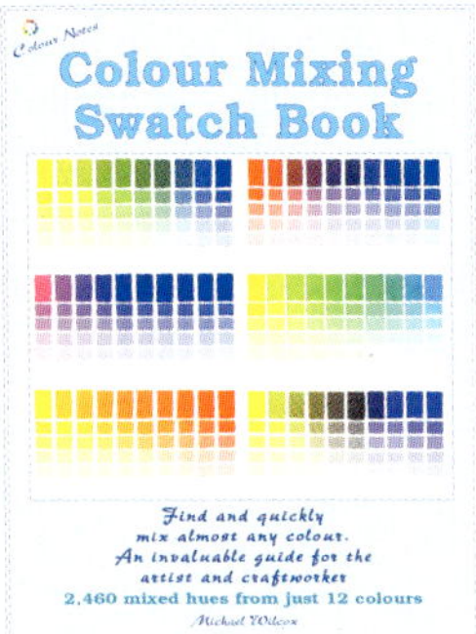

The Michael Wilcox School of Colour Publishing

Artist Quality products created by Artists

SCHOOL OF COLOUR PUBLICATIONS

A range of products has been designed and books and courses published to help bring about a fuller understanding of colour and technique. We offer paints, mixing palettes, books, courses, videos and workbooks.

For further information please contact any of the offices listed below:

The Michael Wilcox School of Color USA
25 Mauchly #328
Irvine
CA 92618 USA
Tel: 949 450 0266
Fax: 949 450 0268
Free Phone: 1888 7 WILCOX
e-mail: wilcoxschool@earthlink.net

The Michael Wilcox School of Colour UK
Gibbet Lane
Whitchurch, Bristol
BS14 0BX
United Kingdom
Tel: 01275 835500
Fax: 01275 892659
e-mail: wilcoxsoc@aol.com

The Michael Wilcox School of Color Australia
PO Box 516
Wanneroo 6946
Western Australia
Tel: (61) 8 9405 6773
Fax: (61) 8 9306 9887
e-mail: wilcoxsoc@iinet.net.au

www.schoolofcolour.com